THE TRUTH MAY BE IN HERE . . .

Did the CIA truly conduct psychic experiments
for their spy program?

Was the work of eccentric scientist Nikola Tesla
deliberately suppressed by the United States government?

Is there life after death?
And is there a way to communicate with the dead?

INVESTIGATING THE UNEXPLAINED

An investigative journalist for over twenty years, **Paul
Roland** has contributed numerous articles to such maga-
zines as *The X Factor, Alien Encounters,* and *Sightings.* His
books include *Revelations—the Wisdom of the Ages, Prophecies
and Predictions, The Complete Guide to Dreams, The Piatkus
Guide to Kabbalah* and *The Piatkus Guide to Angels.*

INVESTIGATING THE
UNEXPLAINED

EXPLORATIONS INTO ANCIENT MYSTERIES, THE PARANORMAL & STRANGE PHENOMENA

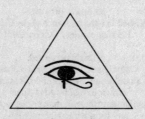

PAUL ROLAND

BERKLEY BOOKS, NEW YORK

INVESTIGATING THE UNEXPLAINED

A Berkley Book / published by arrangement with
Piatkus Books

PRINTING HISTORY
First published in hardcover in 2000 by Piatkus Books
Berkley edition / October 2001

Visit our website at
www.penguinputnam.com

ISBN: 0-425-18200-2

BERKLEY®
Berkley Books are published by The Berkley Publishing Group,
a division of Penguin Putnam Inc.,
375 Hudson Street, New York, New York 10014.
BERKLEY and the "B" design
are trademarks belonging to Penguin Putnam Inc.

PRINTED IN THE UNITED STATES OF AMERICA

10 9 8 7 6 5 4 3 2 1

This book is dedicated to
Karin Page
with love

CONTENTS

PREFACE

THIS IS AN investigation into the unexplained with a difference. In fact, there are several significant differences which I hope distinguish this book from others on a similar theme.

Firstly, I have endeavoured to offer plausible explanations for many of the more extraordinary enigmas that I have examined, rather than compromise with an open verdict which seems to be the fashion these days. I do not see any merit in arguing the case, yet again, for or against the existence of certain phenomena, but instead have concentrated on what the belief in such things reveals about human nature, and what such experiences tell us about the nature of existence. By putting these pieces into a larger picture I hope to take some of the fear out of the unknown.

Secondly, during the course of my research, I personally experienced some of the phenomena that I have described, including psychic surgery, spiritual healing, past life regression and remote viewing, not for the purpose of proving them valid or otherwise, but for the greater understanding that I gained from being "open" to new experiences. Such experiences have left me in no doubt that we are more remarkable beings than we imagine ourselves to be and that we all have the capacity to glimpse the greater reality that exists beyond our physical senses. What appears to be preventing us from discovering our true nature and fulfilling our potential is our preoccupation with the physical world and a reluctance to question the illusions upon which it depends for its existence. When considered in context with the insights that I have obtained through working with intuitives over many years and from studying, teaching and writing about mysticism—in particular, the Jewish mystical tradition known as Kabbalah—I believe that I have acquired an uncommon understanding of certain phenomena which has given me a perspective that a sceptical journalist would be unable to bring to their investigation.

Finally, in order to gather as much evidence as possible and to sift through it with an objective eye I have drawn upon the experience and knowledge of ten experts who are acknowledged authorities in their field. These include the historian Robert Temple, American "psychic spy" David Morehouse, medium and healer Betty Shine, UFO researcher Jenny Randles, science writer Michael White, archaeologist David Hatcher-Childress and the most controversial advocate of the ancient astronaut theory, Erich Von Daniken. Together we unearth some startling artefacts and anomalies which not only question the accepted view of human history, but also shed light on the shadow side of the human psyche.

Although I have divided the book into four distinct subjects they are really only different facets of the same mystery—how we perceive reality and how easily our perception of that reality can be influenced or manipulated by others.

In the first part, I describe some of the many inconsistencies to be found in the orthodox view of human evolution and our understanding of how civilisation developed. In questioning the traditional line with the aid of the explorer and archaeologist David Hatcher-Childress and others I suggest that we may have been conditioned to accept a highly selective and complacent view of history which is going to have to be radically revised in the coming century.

In the second part, the existence of extraterrestrial life is subjected to scrutiny by science writer Michael White, author of *The Science of the X-Files*, and the full range of the alien contact experience is examined with the assistance of UFO expert Jenny Randles. There is a strong possibility that behind the UFO and alien abduction phenomenon there might be something more significant than a purely physical alien presence, something which will shatter our concept of reality.

We create our own image of the world and its workings from what we have been told and we take much of it on trust. But there is increasing reason to believe that our faith has been abused by government agencies with an agenda of their own. As we have become more aware of how easily we can be wilfully misled and deliberately misinformed we have become more cynical as a society and, as such, more receptive to the conspiracy theorists. Part Two ends with a detailed look at one of the most extraordinary yet convincing conspiracy theories—the claim that the Apollo moon landings of the 1960s and 70s were deliberately faked by NASA.

Part Three continues the theme in a different context with a look at the life of the eccentric inventor Nikola Tesla who is said to have been silenced by those with "commercial interests" after having discovered a means of supplying the world with free electricity. This part also features an interview with American psychic spy David Morehouse who claims to have exposed the U.S. government's paradoxical attitude to psychic phenomena—dismissing the conspiracy theorists as paranoid while secretly funding psychic development programmes for military purposes. An examination of the notorious Philadelphia Experiment, which allegedly took place during World War II, suggests that such projects have been on the government's agenda for some considerable time.

The final part focuses on paranormal phenomena, not as examples of supernatural special effects but as expressions of our own innate, natural ability to perceive other realities.

I hope you will find this journey into the unknown as enlightening as I have done.

ACKNOWLEDGMENTS

I am grateful to the following for their contributions to this book: David Hatcher-Childress, David Morehouse, Karin Page, Lynn Picknett, Clive Prince, Betty Shine, Robert Temple, Gregory Van Dyk, Erich Von Daniken and Michael White.

PART ONE

ANCIENT MYSTERIES

The poet T. S. Eliot once remarked, "Humankind cannot bear very much reality," by which he seemed to imply that most of us seek a sense of security in the mundane and routine and are unsettled when our personal vision of the world is challenged.

The following pages present an inventory of extraordinary physical evidence that appears to have been deliberately suppressed because it conflicts with the theories of orthodox science and the academic establishment. The existence of this evidence questions our rather complacent view of human history as a linear progression from "primitive" beginnings to technological and intellectual superiority. It also suggests that we may have subscribed to this highly selective world view because we strongly suspect that we are not the centre of the universe, but need to believe that we are.

1
FORBIDDEN
ARCHAEOLOGY

THE GENERALLY ACCEPTED view of human history states that approximately 4 million years ago, during the Pliocene age, a species of Ramapithecus ape descended from the trees to forage in the grasslands of the African savannah and thereby initiated the process that led to the evolution of modern man. From these ape-like ancestors at least six species of hominids developed forming two distinct groups known as Australopithecus ("southern ape") and Homo ("man"), each existing contemporaneously. Homo habilis is thought to have been the first to use tools and Homo erectus is believed to have become more skilled in their use and also to have discovered the benefits of fire.

But half a million years ago the intellectual capacity of Homo erectus suddenly and inexplicably increased by a third, ensuring that he would prove the superior and win the struggle for survival. Science still cannot account for this quantum leap up the evolutionary ladder, although several theories have been put forward including the widely held view that a meteorite shower might have stimulated a genetic mutation. But if modern man is the result of a mutation is it not more likely that it would have manifested as a physical deformity rather than as a mental attribute?

The human brain has been called the "greatest mystery of all," for with 14,000 million active cells in the cerebral cortex alone not only is it infinitely more complex than any computer that we could currently design, but it appears to have evolved in anticipation of abilities that we have not yet developed. Moreover, the brain does not degenerate as would be expected of any organ which is not used to its capacity. Something beyond a mere physio-biological function animates it, perhaps the same spark which facilitated the jump in consciousness from ape to man.

Whatever the cause, Homo erectus ultimately evolved into Homo sapiens who appeared comparatively recently, about 100,000 years ago, and proved resourceful enough to survive the last Ice Age which ended about 10,000 years ago. At this point the first organised communities came together, walled towns were built in the Jordan Valley and farming replaced hunting as the prime source of sustenance.

This is the timeline to which the scientific establishment subscribes, but hundreds of artefacts discovered over the past 150 years challenge that view and, if verified, may lead to a substantial rewriting of history. These relics suggest that humankind has inhabited the earth for far longer than was previously believed. Moreover, the quality of workmanship and the tools which appear to have been used to make many of these objects have already prompted eminent academics, such as the anthropologist T. Wynn, to conclude that "primitive" man—specifically the Stone Age inhabitants of Tanzania—may have possessed intelligence comparable to ourselves. And if they thought much as we do, is it so unreasonable to assume that they might have achieved more than we have given them credit for?

THE CASE FOR SELECTIVE SELECTION

IT APPEARS THAT the existence of these anomalous artefacts has been known for more than a hundred years, but they have been purposefully ignored by science because they challenge the accepted view of evolution—in much the same way as the massive megalithic monuments of the ancient world have been marginalised merely because we are at a loss to explain their purpose or means of construction.

For 35 years following the publication of Charles Darwin's *Origin of the Species* in 1859 there were many reports of incredible finds, but they had been dismissed out of hand by the scientific establishment because they did not conform to the new orthodoxy. There were stories of a 2-foot-long human-like footprint being found alongside dinosaur tracks in a fossilised rock from the Glenrose River in Texas and of 3,000-year-old stones discovered on the riverbed of the Icka in Peru engraved with what appear to be illustrations of surgery, world maps and dinosaurs. Of course the footprint, which has since been featured in several documentary films, could be a fake and the engravings of supposed surgical operations could instead be depicting human sacrifices. The dinosaurs could be dream beasts and the maps might be imaginary sketches for ritual purposes rather than accurate topographical studies, but there are so many official reports of curious artefacts that it is difficult to easily dismiss them all.

Then in the 1980s an American student, Michael Cremo, and his colleague Richard Thompson, a mathematician and scientist, began research into the history of palaeoanthropology, the study of ancient human relics. They tracked down the original reports of many anomalous artefacts in university libraries from clues found in the footnotes of 19th-century scientific journals and, after eight years of tenacious detective work, they compiled the most intriguing cases in a weighty 900-page study provocatively entitled *Forbidden Archaeology*.

These included details of a carved shell with a human face from the Pleistocene era which had been discovered by Henry Stopes, a Fellow of the Geological Society of England, and a horde of similarly engraved animal bones dated to the Miocene era, 5 million years ago, when there were supposedly no hominids, only apes. This particular discovery was consigned to the archives because the archaeologist concerned, Frank Calvert, was an amateur. In 1872, two years before Calvert unearthed the animal bones, the geologist Edward Charlesworth vainly attempted to persuade fellow members of the Royal Anthropological Society that a cache of shark's teeth which he had unearthed in a layer of soil that was between 2 and 2½ million years old showed unmistakable signs of having been drilled to make a necklace. But his colleagues reminded him that the ape-like Australopithecus was incapable of craftsmanship and they attributed the perfectly spherical holes to parasites and weathering.

More revealing is the story of the Portuguese geologist Carlos Ribeiro who, in the 1860s, discovered "worked flints" in limestone beds in the Tagus River Basin. Ribeiro knew that these beds could be dated to the Pliocene and Miocene era, but in his official report he re-dated his finds as being from the much later Pleistocene period only because he feared that he would be ridiculed if he claimed to have found human artefacts that were evidently between 2 and 5 million years old.

Among Cremo's catalogue of suppressed finds for which he provides documentary proof are a 2-million-year-old detailed figurine from the Plio-Pleistocene age, what appears to be an iron nail discovered in a stone dating to the Devonian era (when we are told the amphibians first appeared) and a metal vase prised from a strata of Precambrian rock in Dorchester, Massachusetts. The Precambrian era is the oldest known geological era which could make a case for the vase being as much as 600 million years old.

Whilst many of the artefacts themselves have vanished into the vaults of various museums leaving only the original reports, a few detailed drawings and the odd photograph, some can still be scrutinised by the determined investigator. For example, in the Museum of Natural History in Klerksdorp, South Africa, there are hundreds of metallic spheres on display which are made from a form of limonite which is so hard that it cannot be scratched by a metallic point, yet many of these spheres have three perfectly parallel grooves which appear to be man-made running around their equator.

Stratigraphic positions (the medium in which the artefacts were found) have also been used to date a mortar and pestle to the Tertiary period (making it between 33 and 55 million years old), a set of clearly identifiable human footprints preserved in volcanic ash to 3.6 million years BCE and a complete human skeleton—comparable anatomically to a modern man—to the Carboniferous period, a staggering 300 million years ago.

Faced with such a wealth of evidence Cremo was forced to conclude that over the past 150 years anthropologists appear to have "buried almost as much evidence as they've dug up" and that this evidence—whether suppressed, ignored or simply forgotten—clearly indicates that human beings like ourselves have co-existed with other creatures for hundreds of millions of years. The evidence is there, but are we perhaps too comfortable in our beliefs to question them?

2

MONUMENTS AND MYSTERIES
OF THE ANCIENT WORLD

THE MASSIVE MONUMENTS of the ancient world continue to inspire not only awe but also wild speculation. Orthodox science admits that it has no ready explanation as to how, for example, technically primitive Peruvians were able to quarry more than 1,000 giant blocks of stone, each weighing up to 120 tonnes, and then transport them to their chosen site at Sacsayhuaman and place them in position with an accuracy that confounds the modern mind. Nor is there a plausible theory to account for the colossal megalithic wall at Ollantaytambo, also in Peru, whose snugly fitting multi-faceted blocks were later copied by the Greek architects of the temple of Apollo in Delphi on a far smaller scale and with much less impressive results.

Another awe-inspiring memorial to ancient ingenuity is the Gateway of the Sun near Puma Punku in Bolivia, which the acknowledged expert on the site, Professor

Arthur Posnansky, has dated to 15,000 BCE. According to historians this was an era when man was only just getting to grips with making spears and creating crude drawings on his cave wall. In contrast to this idea, the Gateway stands at the entrance to a ruined temple in what was once the thriving port city of Tiahuanaco whose wharfs were each wide enough to berth hundreds of ships. The 15-tonne monolith was hewn by unknown means from andesite, one of the hardest stones on earth, with precision cut edges which local legend says were made by a race of giants with access to advanced technology. Unfortunately all traces of the builders and their tools were swept away by a massive flood which struck the region after an earthquake during the construction of the temple between 9,300 and 10,500 BCE. Judging by the crack in the Gateway, the scattered stone blocks which mark the ruins of the city (some weighing up to 440 tonnes) and the discovery of fish fossils and human skeletons 100 feet above nearby Lake Titicaca, the earthquake could have been strong enough to have sunk the legendary "lost continent" of Atlantis, assuming of course that it ever existed.

Similarly, the only explanation that has been put forward to explain the equally imposing temple tower of Ur in Iraq, whose corners are perfectly aligned with the cardinal points of the compass, is that its architects, the Sumerians, were the survivors of a more advanced "lost" civilisation. Although this is a fanciful theory it is nevertheless an inescapable fact that the Sumerians, founders of the first civilisation, appeared fully developed on the stage of history in 4,000 BCE with ready expertise in the construction of architectural features, such as the dome and the arch, that eluded even those master architects of the ancient world, the Egyptians. Although some of Egypt's most awesome artefacts can be accredited to human imagination and ingenuity certain structures continue to defy a rational explanation. Queen Hatshepsut's Obelisk at Karnak, for example, features hundreds of perfectly edged hieroglyphs which modern experts admit they are unable to replicate using the stone and copper tools which the Egyptian stonemasons were thought to have used on the granite column.

THE ENIGMAS EXPLAINED?

RECENTLY, PLAUSIBLE PRACTICAL solutions have been put forward to explain how the pyramids in Egypt, the stone statues of Easter Island and the megalithic stone circle at Stonehenge were constructed by humans as resourceful as ourselves. However, the idea that these and other monuments of antiquity might have been erected using esoteric engineering, or were raised with the assistance of extraterrestrial architects, stubbornly persists.

Esoteric engineering is the term given to techniques which were supposedly used to harness paranormal forces or manipulate the laws of gravity, energy and matter, although no physical evidence has been discovered to substantiate such speculative theories. One example is the technique known as sonic levitation in which initiates of the priesthood are thought to have focused their own mental energy to raise huge blocks of stone and manoeuvre them into place. But no details have been offered to explain how this might have been possible. A similar technique is thought to have been used to focus and store mental energy in a crystal device, similar to a modern laser which would have been used to cut stone.

The Great Pyramid

In the 1990s, after centuries of speculation, a British master builder, Peter Hodges, rejected the generally accepted theory that the pyramid builders at Giza had used mud brick ramps to haul the massive stone blocks into position on the grounds that such a method would have proven impractical. He argued that if this had been the case hundreds of men would have been needed throughout the year which would have seriously inconvenienced the labourers who were local farmers and not slaves as was once believed. Moreover, the ramps would have extended for miles, further even than the quarries from which the stone had been sourced. Instead, Hodges took inspiration from the account recorded by Herodotus in the 5th century BCE in which the Greek historian stated that the blocks had been lifted from tier to tier by mechanical means:

> "The pyramid was built in steps, battlement-wise, as it is called, or according to others, altarwise. After laying the stones for the base they raised the remaining stones by machines formed of short wooden planks. The first machines raised them from the ground to the top of the first step. On this there was another machine which received the stone upon its arrival and conveyed it to the second step, whence a third machine advanced it still higher."

Using a scaled-down model of the pyramid and a succession of levers and packing material to prevent damage to the stones, Hodges and a small team demonstrated that it would have been feasible for the Egyptians to have raised and positioned each block without recourse to magical means or extraterrestrial assistance, provided that they did so before the casing stones were added.

Despite this explanation there are many who still doubt that human beings could have manoeuvred the 2½ million blocks under any means; more masonry, in fact, than is contained in all the chapels, churches and medieval cathedrals of Europe added together.

Stonehenge

Forty years earlier Stonehenge had presented Professor Tom Lethbridge of Cambridge University with a different problem, for the 79 bluestones, each weighing 5 tonnes, which comprise the outer circle and the horseshoe, had been hewn from diorite, a dark, course-grained igneous plutonic rock, of which there were no deposits within 130 miles of Salisbury Plain.

Again, the solution was found in the past. Bishop Geoffrey of Monmouth, who died in 1155, recorded a local legend which stated that the bluestones had been taken from a circle known as the Giant's Dance at Killaraus in Ireland. With this modest clue Lethbridge deduced that Killaraus must refer to a settlement near Tipperary, for Killaraus translates as "the church on the River Ary" and Tipperary is situated by the River Ary near a quarry of diorite. From there the stones could have been taken downriver to the sea at Waterford and carried across to the mouth of the River Avon roped between two ships in the style of a particular type of anchor known as a kedge. With the water taking the weight, it would be comparatively easy to navigate to within a few miles of Salisbury Plain from where the stones could be eased on to a sledge, dragged up to the site and levered into position. The lintels would have been

raised during the winter months when the builders could
guarantee a heavy fall of snow on Salisbury Plain with
which they could make temporary ramps. Once hauled into
position each lintel would be secured by a mortice and
tenon joint, the bulb of the lintel fitting snugly into the cup
which had been carved out of the upright.

Again, however, such a logical explanation continues to
be discounted by those seeking a more exotic solution to
the ancient enigma.

Easter Island

According to the controversial writer Erich Von Daniken,
the most enthusiastic advocate of the ancient astronaut theory, the features of the statues which stand as silent sen-
tinels on Easter Island in the Pacific Ocean are those of
extraterrestrials who had been marooned on earth in
ancient times. Archaeologists prefer the idea that they represent the islanders' ancestors and suggest that they were
moved into position using wooden sledges. The only problem with this theory is that the island is treeless and some
of the statues stand up to 10 metres in height and weigh up
to 82 tonnes. Without some form of rolling platform it is
difficult to imagine how they could have been transported
from the inland quarries.

It was not until the 1990s that a team of botanists came
up with the answer. Pollen analysis revealed that the island
was once thick with trees and that when these had all been
cut down the quarrying ceased, leaving some of the sculp-
tures unfinished. With their natural resources depleted and
the animal habitat devastated, the islanders abandoned
their home bequeathing another mystery to confound the
experts.

THESE PROSAIC EXPLANATIONS may not be as dramatic as those proposed by the ancient astronaut enthusiasts, but they stand up to scrutiny and, more importantly, they credit our ancestors with a range of remarkable skills and technical knowledge, which demonstrates that technology evolves according to the needs of each culture.

Our reluctance to credit a pre-industrial people with skills which we do not possess ourselves is understandable. We have been conditioned to think of the ancients as superstitious primitives who erected massive monuments to house the corpses of their kings or to make human sacrifices to their gods. But these assumptions are now seen to be largely without foundation.

THE MIRROR OF HEAVEN

"WHATEVER IS BELOW is like that which is above and whatever is above is like that which is below." This central maxim from the *Corpus Hermeticum*, one of the most sacred texts of the ancient world, summed up a spiritual view of the universe which was shared by such distant and diverse civilisations as the Maya, the Egyptians, the Celts, the Hindus, the Greeks and the Semitic tribes in the centuries before Christianity. The belief that our physical world is a reflection of a celestial realm, to which our immortal souls return after death, became the foundation of classical Greek philosophy, Judaic mysticism and the Egyptian cult of the dead, as well as the Pagan practices of the Druids and the teachings of Buddhism. And there is now sound archaeological evidence that this shared view of the structure of existence and of the immortality of the soul may actually have inspired the construction of many of the wonders of the ancient world. Furthermore, these secrets may originally have come from that single source, the more spiritually and technologically advanced pre–Ice Age civilisation: the lost continent of Atlantis.

THE SHADOW SERPENT

IT APPEARS THAT many ancient monuments were constructed with precision and purpose, the most significant sites being astronomically aligned to emphasise the union between heaven and earth. For example, the Mayan city of Chichen Itza on Mexico's Yucatan peninsula incorporates measurements corresponding to the astronomical calendar, which demonstrates their architects' advanced understanding of astronomy.

The narrow windows and doors of the domed observatory provide precise sight lines for the study of significant celestial events such as the setting of Venus at its southerly and northerly extremes, and for predicting the sunset at the equinoxes.

American engineer Hugh Harleston Jr. made over 9,000 on-site measurements at Chichen Itza in order to prove that the many pyramid-like structures incorporated a standard unit of measure (1.05946 metres) which enabled all key dimensions to be expressions of multiples of 72. The significance of this number derives from the Maya's need to predict the precession of the equinoxes for ritual purposes. Precession is an astronomical phenomenon caused by a shift in the earth's axis which results in notable dates, such as the equinoxes, aligning themselves to different signs of the zodiac over a prolonged period of time. The significance of the numbers 72 in precessional terms is as follows: 72 is the number of years required for one degree of precession, the motion of the earth which slows the Sun's arrival at a specific stellar "address." From this information the Maya created a calendar of such unerring accuracy that they were able to use it to predict the solar eclipse which occurred over Mexico City in 1991.

In addition to these discoveries Harleston noted that each pyramid has 91 steps leading to a summit platform. When the total number of steps plus the platform are added together they make 365, the number of days in the solar year. He also observed that the principal axis running through each pyramid from south-east to north-west was deliberately offset by 15 degrees and 30 minutes to the east and west of true north-south. This was to target the rising sun on the winter and summer solstices so that on these two days the setting sun creates a serpent-shaped silhouette which appears to slither up the steps towards the summit. This effect was contrived by the Maya to honour the snake god Kukulkan (Quetzalcat, the "plumed serpent" god of the Incas) to whom they dedicated each temple.

Although the celestial symbolism of such sites is only now becoming common knowledge thanks to the work of "alternative" historians such as Graham Hancock, John Anthony West and Robert Bauval, it has in fact been recorded for decades. According to American academic Stansbury Hagar, who carried out an extensive study of the site in the 1920s, the principal axis of Chichen Itza, known in some traditions as "the way of the stars," was designed to represent the Milky Way. As such it would serve as a symbolic path for the transmigration of souls from earth to heaven. But unknown to Hagar this was not the only site which attempted to consummate the marriage of heaven and earth.

AS ABOVE, SO BELOW

ONE NIGHT IN November 1983, while on an expedition in the Saudi Arabian desert, the Belgian construction engineer and amateur Egyptologist Robert Bauval awoke from a restless sleep. He had been struggling with one of Egypt's most inexplicable enigmas: the third of the three pyramids at Giza is considerably smaller than its companions although Pharaoh Menkaura, for whom it was designed, was of equal stature to his predecessors. But equally odd is the fact that this third pyramid is out of line with the other two, though all three had been aligned with the four cardinal points of the compass with painstaking precision. Bauval reasoned that the anomalies must have been intentional, and if so, what could they signify?

As he gazed up at the stars he was joined by a friend who pointed out in passing that the three stars of Orion's belt—Zeta, Epsilon and Delta—were not in perfect alignment; the third and smallest star was offset to the east. At that, Bauval was struck by a realisation as profound as a mystic's vision. The Giza pyramids were evidently intended to symbolise these stars which are known to have had mystical significance for the ancient Egyptians. They believed that the constellation of Orion was the home of their god Osiris who waited to welcome the souls of the pharaohs who were themselves considered incarnations of the god. Moreover, the three pyramids must have been built at precisely this spot on the bank of the Nile to mimic their proximity to the Milky Way which looks like a glistening river in the night sky.

In a fever of excitement Bauval made comparisons with other sites in the region and discovered that the pyramid at Zawyat al-Aryan corresponds to the star at Orion's right shoulder while the pyramid of Nebka at Abu Ruwash corresponds to the foot of the celestial figure. Unfortunately, there was no trace of the two more pyramids needed to complete the pattern. Perhaps more pressing needs prevented them from being built, or maybe they still await discovery beneath the desert sand.

Using a computer sky map programme to simulate the night sky as it appeared in ancient times, Bauval pinned down precisely when this particular mirroring of ground and sky last occurred, with the stars identically disposed in relation to the meridian, and was given the date 10,500 BCE.

This, he reasoned, could be the era which ancient texts refer to as Zep Tepi, or the first time, and which they describe as being a Golden Age when men walked with the gods. But rather than being merely a myth could this Golden Age possibly commemorate the date when Egypt was founded, and if so, by whom?

IN SEARCH OF THE "FIRST TIME"

THIS BRINGS US back to the possibility that Egypt and other advanced cultures of the ancient world, such as the Sumerian and the Mayan, may have been established by the survivors of an earlier, technically superior civilisation which existed before the last Ice Age. In the course of researching his book, *Heaven's Mirror*, and a TV series,

Quest for the Lost Civilisation, English author and investigator Graham Hancock compared the measurements and layouts of a number of significant sites around the world and made startling discoveries of his own.

The outwardly contrasting cultures of Egypt, Cambodia and Mexico shared a common belief in the immortality of the soul, all three used pyramids in their sacred architecture and they all demonstrated an advanced knowledge of astronomy. But, more significantly, they all aspired to the heavens which they considered the home of the soul and they aligned their monuments with specific stars to which they believed their souls would return after death. The southern shaft in the Queen's Chamber of the Great Pyramid at Giza, for example, is targeted at Sirius, the star which the Egyptian identified with the goddess Isis, while the southern shaft in the King's Chamber targets Zeta Orionis, the brightest star in Orion's belt, representing Isis' husband, Osiris. It is now thought that the Great Pyramid was built not to house the Pharaoh's body, but to initiate novice priests into the mysteries of existence.

Hancock was initially inspired by the work of an American academic, Dr. Eleanor Maneka, who discovered that the ancient architects of the temple complex at Angkor in Cambodia had used a standard unit of measurement, the cubit, in its construction, which is scaled to cycles of time that are integral to Hindu belief. For example, the main causeway is 1,728 cubits in length which corresponds to the 1,728,000-year-long first stage in Hindu cosmology. Other primary avenues mark the lengths of subsequent ages. Again, precessional numbers feature in the alignments and dimensions of the temples. There are 72 temples and the causeway at Angkor Wat is three-quarters of a degree offset due east. In precessional terms this corresponds to 54 years, a figure found all over the two sites (54 is considered a significant precessional number being half of 108. It is part of a sequence of precessional numbers 54, 72, 108, 144, 180, 216 . . . and so on). Hancock says that the offset gave the priests a three-day warning of the spring equinox, a day when the sun lines up with the central tower to spectacular effect. Nearby, the temple complex of Angkor Thom boasts 54 towers which are connected by a bridge featuring 54 mythical figures representing the forces of light and darkness. Their eternal struggle is thought to be symbolic of the mechanics of precession which the Hindus envisaged as a contest between giants for control of the earth.

During the course of his own researches Hancock discovered another fascinating fact. The ground plan of the temple complex at Angkor matched stars in the constellation of Draco (the Dragon) as it appeared in the night sky in 10,500 BCE. This date, he believes, is highly significant because it is thought to be the year when the lost continent of Atlantis was sent to the bottom of the sea in the aftershock of a natural catastrophe. He argues that from this fact it is reasonable to speculate that the survivors might have migrated to emerging centres of civilisation such as Egypt and Cambodia where they used their superior knowledge to raise the monuments which all form part of a grand design. This seems even more likely when one learns that the leonine-shaped Sphinx was aligned with the constellation of Leo in that fateful year and together all four crucial constellations corresponded with the four cardinal points of the compass at dawn on the spring equinox in 10,500 BCE. Aquarius was setting due west, Leo was rising due east, due south lay Orion and due north was Draco.

Hancock contends that it is no coincidence that Giza and Angkor are separated by precisely 72 degrees of longitude and he suggests that it is only a matter of time before we discover a fourth sacred site dedicated to the constellation of Aquarius at equal distance from the others.

There are several contenders for this fourth site including Tiahuanaco in Bolivia whose central axis is thought to have been flooded to mirror the Milky Way. This water symbolism may be significant for water is, of course, the symbol of Aquarius.

Another is to be found beneath the sparkling surface of the waters which lap the southernmost shore of Japan. Here, archaeologists are currently studying the ruins of what appears to be an ancient temple which, if proven beyond doubt to be man-made, will qualify it as the oldest known construction in the world. This massive stone structure is thought to have sunk beneath the waves in the wake of a natural catastrophe over 10,000 years ago making it a prime contender.

IN SEARCH OF ATLANTIS

ORTHODOX SCIENCE AND the academic establishment have always been dismissive of the suggestion that Atlantis was anything other than an idyllic setting for Plato's (427–347 BCE) political parable *Critias*. Serious historians believe the legend of Atlantis is no more than a fanciful moral fable pieced together by Plato from stories he had heard during his childhood, and may have been inspired in part by the eruption of the Santorin volcano which devastated Minoan Crete in 1,500 BCE. But the re-dating of the Sphinx (see p. 25) and the recent discovery that an ancient seafaring nation may have mapped areas of the world thousands of years before the earliest surviving charts were made has forced them to think again.

In 1956, the American academic Charles Hapgood rediscovered a number of 16th-century maps which clearly show features that were thought not to have been charted until over 300 years later. Hapgood immediately noticed that a chart dating from 1513 belonging to the Turkish admiral Piri Reis showed the eastern coastline of South America and part of Antarctica that historians had thought were still to be discovered. He submitted the map for examination by U.S. Air Force experts who concluded that it was accurate to within half a degree:

> "This indicates the coastline [of Antarctica] had been mapped before it was covered by the ice cap. The ice cap in this region is now about a mile thick. We have no idea how the data on this map can be reconciled with the state of geographical knowledge in 1513."

Hapgood believed it was because Piri Reis had based his chart on those drawn up by this ancient seafaring nation. Further confirmation came when he chanced across another map copied in 1531 for Oronteus Finaeus, a 16th-century map maker, which detailed the fertile plains, ice-free rivers and mountains of Antarctica, a continent not "officially'" discovered until 1820. These features, some of which had been described by Plato, were to be found on the 1949 survey—made by a multi-national expedition (Norway, Sweden and Britain), who took sonar soundings to map topographical details beneath the ice. Furthermore, scientists have recently revealed that an examination of ice core samples has confirmed that there were freeflowing rivers in the region detailed on the Oronteus Finaeus map as recently as 4,000 BCE.

This may suggest that the lost continent was a reality. We even have an idea as to how the people might have looked from ancient sculptured heads found in Central America that cannot be linked to any indigenous tribe there. The Olmecs, as they are called, boast features that are uncharacteristic of the indigenous population, and also bear a striking resemblance to the features of the Sphinx on the Giza plateau . . .

Of course, there is still no conclusive proof that this lost civilisation was technically advanced in anything other than astronomy, navigation and cartography or that the people possessed esoteric secrets which they subsequently entrusted to the emerging cultures of Egypt and Sumeria. But it is surely enough to stimulate a reassessment of our accepted view of history.

3

RE-DATING THE SPHINX

THE GREAT SPHINX, guardian of the pyramids at Giza, is one of the wonders of the ancient world. It is not only the largest stone statue ever built, but also a symbol of the enigma that is Egypt and of its many mysteries which still hold a strange fascination for us today. With the recent discovery that the statue may be as much as 12,000 years old—10,000 years older than historians had thought—there has been much speculation that the land of the pharaohs may have been founded by the survivors of a far more ancient civilisation.

CLIMATIC CLUES

MUCH RESEARCH INTO the true origin and age of the Sphinx has been done by American Egyptologist John Anthony West whose interest in ancient mysteries was fired by the writings of the 19th-century philosopher and

mathematician Rene Schwaller de Lubicz, the first academic to question the age of the Sphinx. West is a controversial figure, a self-taught Egyptologist with a reputation for
challenging the traditionalists and questioning what he
considers to be their complacency. They in turn dismiss his
theories as purely speculative, and having no basis in fact.
Consequently, he made extra efforts to ensure that his
Sphinx theories had a sound scientific foundation and persuaded Dr. Robert Schoch, an eminent academic geologist
from Boston University, to examine the body of the statue
for evidence of water erosion.

After the last Ice Age, about 12,000 BCE, Egypt
became a lush tropical paradise with heavy rainfall. It was
only comparatively recently that its climate changed to the
dry, arid desert that we are familiar with today. If Dr.
Schoch could find evidence of water erosion it would
mean that the monument pre-dated dynastic Egypt which
was established around 4,000 BCE. It would also demonstrate that there had been an advanced race with engineering skills thousands of years before the invention of the
wheel.

As West suspected, Schoch found unmistakable signs of
water erosion on the body of the Sphinx and along the
walls that surround it. But the weathering was uneven,
suggesting that it might have been carved over a prolonged
period beginning at a time when Egypt was subtropical
and ending when it was dry. Schoch was certain that the
Sphinx is far older than the archaeological establishment
will accept—perhaps 8,500 years old—but he refused to
risk his reputation in speculating who might have built it
or why.

THE FACE OF THE SPHINX

EVEN THE MOST conservative archaeologists agree that the Sphinx is far older than the pyramids at Giza, although they date it no earlier than the reign of Pharaoh Khafre who ruled from 2,520 to 2,494 BCE. The accepted view was that Khafre had commissioned the statue to be built in his image, but a comparison between the weathered features of the monument and those of the Pharaoh's face (taken from a statue in the Cairo Museum) revealed significant discrepancies which could not be accounted for by natural erosion or vandalism. (Vandalism is not a modern epidemic. Monuments to heretical pharaohs were routinely desecrated by their successors and those that survived were sometimes used as target practice by conquering armies. Until the comparatively recent introduction of preservation orders, further damage was done by the locals who regularly robbed the tombs and temples of their ancestors for building materials.)

Using anatomically accurate sketches of both faces, Lieutenant Domingo, a senior forensic artist from the New York Police Department, found that the Sphinx's eyes were set further back and its jaw was considerably more pronounced than the Pharaoh's. Even allowing for the possibility that the Sphinx may have been an idealised portrait of Khafre, Domingo was in no doubt that the faces were of two separate individuals. The fact is that the jutting jaw of the Sphinx makes the face anything but ideal. It is almost ape-like in appearance which no pharaoh would have found flattering. The belief that Khafre built the Sphinx hangs on the fact that the Pharaoh's cartouche (the relief bearing his name in hieroglyphics), can be seen on the stela between the paws. However, it now seems more likely that this inscription commemorates the restoration of the statue which Khafre had ordered to be carried out in his name. Dr. Schoch reasoned that Khafre had attempted to renovate the Sphinx and the surrounding temples knowing that they were the monuments of an earlier era, believing that in doing so he would be adopting the site for his dynasty and finding favour with the gods of the Nile. Khafre's refurbishments were quite distinct from the original work. He had covered the limestone with granite slabs and he may also have been responsible for having the head re-carved along more Egyptian lines which has resulted in it being disproportionate to the body.

This poses the question: if the face is not that of an Egyptian pharaoh, what is it? Schoch used computer projections to remodel the head in proportion to the rest of the body and completed the broken lines and restored the mutilated features. His conclusion was that it is not the figure of a man, but of an animal, most likely a lion. This ties in with the fact that the statue was aligned with the constellation of Leo as it appeared on the spring equinox in 10,500 BCE (see page 21). Seismography specialist Dr. Thomas Dobecki was invited to analyse the rock and give an educated estimate for the date when it was carved. His findings confirmed that the Sphinx had been shaped over a protracted period with the face pre-dating the rear of the body by as much as 3,000 years. During subsequent sound mapping tests Dr. Dobecki discovered the existence of tunnels and a large chamber 5 metres below the paws of the Sphinx, the uniform shape and dimensions of which lead him to conclude that it must be man-made.

SECRET CHAMBERS

ALTHOUGH THE EXISTENCE of the tunnels and secret chamber was only confirmed in 1995 by Dobecki, their discovery had been predicted 60 years earlier by the celebrated psychic Edgar Cayce (see page 202). Cayce, who was known as the "sleeping prophet" because of his tendency to lapse into a trance when making his uncannily accurate predictions, claimed to have recollections of his previous lives in dynastic Egypt. From these "memories" he learnt that the Sphinx had been built by survivors of Atlantis.

Evidence of this ancient, lost civilisation is thought to be hidden in the chamber which remains to be explored. It is hoped that when permission is finally obtained for an excavation, archaeologists will uncover a library of archaic wisdom that will shed light on some of the world's oldest mysteries.

NOT SURPRISINGLY, THE Egyptian academic establishment view West and his team's revisionist approach as a personal attack upon their authority and against their cultural heritage, and have responded strongly. Dr. Zahi Hawass, Director General of the Giza Pyramids counters West's controversial claims by saying that they "represent nothing but a continuation of the cultural invasion of Egypt's civilisation." West has gone on record as saying that he views such resistance and hostility as inevitable as he is challenging "entrenched ideas." He adds: "This means the establishment is going to battle it to the death.

In effect, what we are doing is upsetting the apple cart and these people make a living selling apples."

The geological evidence, and time itself, appears to be against Dr. Hawass.

4

ALIEN ARTEFACTS

HIDDEN AMONG THE exhibits of the Istanbul Archaeological Museum in Turkey is what appears to be a sculpted scale replica of a single-seat spacecraft complete with a headless astronaut. Local press reports claimed this could be as much as 3,000 years old. The initial reports stated that it had been unearthed during routine excavations at Toprakkale (the site of the ancient city of Tuspa), and they included a brief description of the artefact with a photograph which clearly showed the "pilot" sitting with his knees to his chest dressed in a ribbed spacesuit, boots and gloves. If genuine, it would offer conclusive physical proof that the earth had been visited by extraterrestrials thousands of years ago. However the museum insists that it is a modern hoax and initially refused to put the object on display. Curiously, when news of the find leaked out the curator, Dr. Esin Eren, and the director, Dr. Alpay Pasinli, gave conflicting explanations as to how it had come into their possession. At first they said that it had been confiscated from a tourist who had attempted to smuggle it through customs. Then in answer to another inquiry they claimed that in 1973 it had been brought in by a dealer who had asked for it to be authenticated, but who did not return after he learnt that it was a fake. Neither Dr. Eren nor Dr. Pasinli explained why they had allowed a supposedly fake artefact to be catalogued and placed in the vaults. Nor could they comment on why none of the staff had bothered to make a note of the dealer's name and address. In fact, the official reason for believing it to be a fake was singularly unscientific.

"It does not reflect the era's style, the era from which it supposedly comes," a museum spokesman has been quoted as saying. "It looks like a space capsule, but of course there were no such things at that time. So someone has allowed himself a practical joke . . ." However, when the biblical scholar Zecharia Sitchin visited the museum in 1997 he examined the object thoroughly and concluded that it was unlikely to be a fake. It was certainly light, but it could have been made from volcanic ash stone. The museum insisted that it had been cast in plaster from a mould made from a plastic toy, but Sitchin noted that the neck of the astronaut is the same colour as the rest of the object. If it had been plaster it would have revealed the unmistakable whiteness of the material when the head was broken off. Secondly, Sitchin remarks that toys tend to be replicas of real objects, yet neither NASA nor the Russian space programme developed a one-seat cockpit rocket without wings or even a tail in the 1970s when the object was allegedly manufactured.

Still Dr. Pasinli was reluctant to draw visitors' attention to this controversial acquisition for the reason that he knew of no other relics of this kind from antiquity. To his astonishment Sitchin was able to supply him with dozens of what appear to be illustrations of wingless spacecraft from the Americas and the Near East and as a result, the headless spaceman is now on public display.

A CATALOGUE OF CURIOSITIES

THE NUMBER OF "alien" artefacts is indeed considerable.

A 3,000-year-old ceramic figure found on the Bolivian border models what looks like a helmeted spacesuit, although it could be a deep-sea diving suit, which would not make it any less remarkable.

On the other side of the world a 5,000-year-old Japanese Dogu sculpture is on display wearing what appears to be a helmet and goggles. This invites comparison with strikingly similar images depicted in cave paintings created by Australian Aborigines during the same period, and the ancient inhabitants of Tassili, North Africa, in 6,000 BCE. The same helmeted figures appear in prehistoric rock carvings near Capo di Ponte in Italy and in Peruvian petroglyphs of indeterminable age.

Excavations in Nepal unearthed a carved dish from 2,000 BCE which seems to record an extraterrestrial visit. In the centre of the plate is a symbol of the sun from which an elliptical flying saucer shape emerges. On the rim are runic letters, a pair of many tentacled creatures and a humanoid figure with a head that is disproportionate to its body in the image of the alien species known commonly as the Greys.

A Neolithic cave painting in south-west France has proven equally puzzling as it depicts an upright humanoid

figure with a tail who is in communication with what looks
suspiciously like three UFOs.

More "flying machines" figure on the ceiling of the
temple of Abydos in Egypt. In fact, they are so unmistak-
ably characteristic of a helicopter and other military hard-
ware that one automatically assumes that they are part of
an elaborate hoax, yet they have been authenticated by
experts as having been carved in 3,000 BCE.

Other recently recovered out-of-place relics, as they are
known, have no obvious extraterrestrial connection but
they are certainly unusual.

The Baghdad Battery

In Iraq in 1938 Austrian archaeologist Dr. Wilhelm Konig
unearthed one of the most puzzling artefacts of the pre-
Christian era stored in the basement of the Baghdad
museum whose combination of components suggests that
it may have been an early example of a battery cell. It is a
6-inch clay pot containing a slender 5-inch copper cylinder
soldered with tin alloy. The cylinder, which is sealed with
a copper disc at one end and insulated with asphalt at the
other, contains an iron rod which has evidently been
corroded with acid. Konig commissioned a replica to be
made and fruit juice substituted for battery acid. The result
was enough power to electroplate jewellery with silver or
gold, a process which was thought to have been a modern
invention. However, the Baghdad Battery, as it is known,
dates from approximately 248 BCE. Elsewhere among the
exhibits, Konig discovered copper vases electroplated with
silver which had been excavated from sites in southern
Iraq. These he believed were of Sumerian origin making
them at least 4,500 years old.

Egyptian Electricity

In Egypt, where one would expect to see tomb walls illustrated with spells to assist the dead on their journey through the Underworld, there are murals which baffle even the most experienced Egyptologists.

In a chamber of the Late Ptolemaic Temple of Hathor at Dendera there is a panel showing a number of priests holding oblong tubes, in each of which can be seen a serpent. The Swedish engineer Henry Kjellson, author of *Disappeared Technology*, reveals that the hieroglyphs refer to these snakes as "seref," which means "to glow," suggesting an electrical energy source. If so, this source may be in a box on which the god Atum-Ra is seated, for what appears to be a braided cable runs from the box to the tubes. According to electromagnetics expert, Alfred D. Bielek, the curious pillar on which the priests are resting the tubes is a high-voltage insulator. Elsewhere in the temple other scenes depict men and women sitting beneath the tubes holding out their hands as if receiving some form of radiation treatment.

Egyptian Aeroplanes

In 1898, five years before the Wright brothers made the first powered flight, a wooden model of a strange-looking bird was found in the tomb of Pa-di-Imen in north Saqqara. For the next 70 years it lay among a collection of figurines in the local museum until archaeologist and model plane enthusiast, Dr. Kahlil Messiha, singled it out for closer examination. He immediately recognised certain features, such as the aerodynamic wings and a separate rudder which slots on to the tail, as being characteristic of a mod-

ern glider. Though his colleagues greeted his discovery
with incredulity Dr. Messiha demonstrated the 2,000-year-
old model's air worthiness by launching it in the time-
honoured fashion. To his delight it glided a considerable
distance before making a perfect landing.

Messiha was intrigued by the fact that the ancient Egyptians often built scale models of treasured possessions to
place in their tombs and he wondered if there might have
been a full-sized version, assuming that the glider was not
merely a child's toy. According to his calculations a full-
scale version might have travelled at up to 65 miles an
hour and carried considerable loads, although he could
only speculate as to what the method of propulsion might
have been.

The Colombian Concorde

Another "ancient aircraft" came into the hands of biologist–
zoologist Ivan T. Sanderson in 1969. It was an official
replica cast from a Colombian artefact which had been
worn as a pendant in the first century by a member of the
Sinu people, a race pre-dating the Incas. Sanderson immediately recognised that it had mechanical rather than animal features. The wings are delta-shaped, unlike those of a
bird, and the rudder is a right-angled upright tail fin like
that of a fish, although there is no fish which does not have
a counter-balancing fin. After consulting a number of aero-
nautical experts, including Dr. Arthur Poyslee of the Aero-
nautical Institute of New York, Sanderson was forced to
conclude that it is a model of a high-speed aircraft. But
perhaps the most curious detail is the unmistakable imprint
of the Hebrew letter *beth*, or B, which can be seen on the
left face of the rudder where modern aircraft have their

insignia. This indicates that it may have originated in the Middle East and yet historians deny that trade, or indeed travel of any kind, existed between these lands at that time. Of course, crossing such vast distances would have been purely routine in an aircraft.

5

LOST CIVILISATIONS

PROLIFIC AMERICAN AUTHOR, adventurer and explorer David Hatcher-Childress has hacked his way through the steaming jungles of the world, crossed searing desert sands and climbed windswept mountains in search of lost civilisations and ancient mysteries, and in so doing has acquired the reputation of being the real Indiana Jones.

David is the perfect example of that all too rare species—a highly educated, knowledgeable and credible expert with his head in the clouds, but his feet planted firmly on the ground.

> "I've been fascinated by the idea of alien artefacts, ancient science and psychic phenomena since childhood. I've always been intrigued by what couldn't be explained, but I've maintained a strict scientific approach as a balance to all my investigations. At university in the mid-70s I was regularly winning science awards, but I was also becoming increasingly suspicious of big business and the role

corporations appeared to be playing in keeping the whole truth from the public. The turning point was when I started reading so-called radical theories on the Kennedy assassination. After that I couldn't subscribe to the accepted view of history ever again."

In his numerous books and magazine articles David acts as an unofficial guide to long lost civilisations which have been sidelined by history.

According to various esoteric sources, which David considers reliable, the first civilisation was established 78,000 years ago on a continent known as Lemuria or Mu where the science of government was developed to a sophisticated degree. The area is believed to have been devastated by an earthquake in approximately 24,000 BCE caused by a shift in the earth's magnetic poles, leaving the ruins of huge megalithic buildings still to be discovered in the Pacific.

It is said that the destruction of Lemuria drained the oceans of the world as water rushed into the newly formed Pacific Basin leaving the islands in the Atlantic high and dry. In time these merged with the Poseid Archipelago of the Atlantic Ocean to form a small continent which has been mythologised as Atlantis, though its real name, according to David's exhaustive researches, was Poseid. The Atlanteans (or Poseideans) are believed to have developed technology far in advance of that which exists on our planet today.

"Whilst we can only speculate as to the wonders of Lemuria and Atlantis the ancient texts of India's Rama Empire have been preserved to give us detailed descriptions of one of the earliest empires on earth. In the past century the considerably sophisticated cities of Mohenjo Daro (Mound of the Dead) and Harappa have been discovered in the Indus Valley of modern-day Pakistan forcing archaeologists to push the dates for the origin of Indian civilisation back thousands of years. Archaeologists believe that these cities were conceived as a whole before being built, and were astounded to discover that the plumbing and sewage systems were superior to those found in most modern cities in Asia.

"It is thought that when Atlantis and Rama were thriving, the Mediterranean was a large and fertile valley inhabited by a civilisation known as the Osirians. When Atlantis was destroyed the Atlantic flooded the Mediterranean Basin, destroying the Osirians' great cities and forcing them to relocate to higher ground. This scenario explains the existence of the 200 sunken cities which have been identified throughout the Mediterranean.

"I think it is quite possible that the Egyptian, Minoan and Mycenean civilisations could be remnants of this ancient culture which is thought to have created an early form of electrical power and to have invented a sophisticated transport system, like those of Rama and Atlantis. If anyone thinks this sounds far-fetched they should study the mysterious cart tracks of Malta, which go over cliffs and under water, as if they were once part of an ancient Osirian tram-line, perhaps for carrying quarried stone to cities that are now submerged.

"Another example of the high technology of the Osirians is the awesome stone platform at Ba'albek in Lebanon. The main platform is comprised of the largest hewn rocks in the world, the famous ashlars of Ba'albek, some of which are 82 feet long, 15 feet thick and are estimated to weigh between 1,200 and 1,500 tonnes each!"

David's favourite "lost cause" is Nan Madol, a 28-square kilometre megalithic city which lies off the coast of the Micronesian island of Pohnpei on a man-made island containing over 250 million tonnes of prismatic basalt salt. Most of the city is now underwater, but it is still possible to navigate part of its vast network of artificial canals which have earned it the title, Venice of the Pacific. Nan Madol was discovered by Europeans in the early years of the 19th century and its wonders were recorded by the German archaeologist Johann Stanislaus Kubary whose manuscript was accidentally burnt by one of his four native wives! Kubary also plundered the island's secret stores of treasure and priceless relics, but the ship carrying the booty sank off the Marshall Islands and is unlikely to be recovered.

In the 1930s another German archaeologist, Herbert Rittlinger, published an account of his researches in the region, noting that it had once been "a brilliant and splendid centre of a celebrated kingdom that had existed there untold millennia ago." Rittlinger repeated the legends of fabulous treasure which pearl divers and Chinese merchants had searched for in secret on the seabed, and the tales that they had returned with. These described how the divers had explored submerged streets where the remains of the houses bear plaques inscribed with the names of the inhabitants. The divers also found monoliths, stone vaults and pillars which are now encrusted with mussels and coral. Rittlinger also recorded the efforts of the Japanese who, just prior to World War II, stripped the sunken House of the Dead of its "platinum coffins" although no platinum exists on the island. The Japanese also recovered human remains which indicated that the inhabitants had been over 2 metres tall—giants by the standards of the region.

Later expeditions found shards of pottery which ther-moluminescence tests confirmed are more than 2,000 years old, yet the natives of Pohnpei have never used pot-tery. David has visited the site many times and been impressed by its 10-metre-high walls constructed from giant basalt logs each weighing about 20 tonnes and rocks weighing up to 50 tonnes apiece. But what haunts him is the eerie silence which has prompted him to describe the overgrown ruins and inlets as "a city of spirits."

Neither the experts nor the natives have been able to offer an explanation as to how the massive blocks—many weighing more than those of the Great Pyramid in Egypt—were carried over the mountainous terrain of Pohnpei to the coast. The fact that the locals now live in grass huts on the mainland suggests that the culture regressed, perhaps after a natural catastrophe which made the city unsafe for habitation. If so, it is possible that the same decline occurred during other eras elsewhere in the world leaving ruins but no record of the technology which made them possible.

EXTRATERRESTRIAL ARCHAEOLOGY

IN ADDITION TO revealing what he believes to be the hid-den history of humankind David also makes a more plau-sible case for the existence of extraterrestrials than the interventionists Erich Von Daniken or Alan F. Alford do, because he has no preconceived ideas which he is eager to prove. His approach is to simply present the evidence (invariably in the form of official space agency pho-tographs, ancient texts and monuments) and leave the reader to draw the obvious and inescapable conclusions.

For example, in his book *Extraterrestrial Archaeology*, the "evidence" consists of masses of official NASA and Russian space agency photographs of which the most startling is a series of NASA shots clearly showing two objects moving across the surface of the moon leaving tread trails in their wake.

> "That's one of my favourite shots. The sequence clearly shows one of these objects moving upwards out of a crater, then back down the crater rim and moving along contrary to the laws of nature and lunar atmospherics. And yet the NASA guys still insist on calling these objects 'rolling rocks'! They studied them and admitted that they couldn't explain how the objects could do that, but even with the evidence in front of their faces they still wouldn't come to the conclusion that these were self-propelled machines. Such possibilities couldn't appear in their official papers."

Similarly startling are the photographs of what are known as the Blair Cuspids—a geometrical alignment of obelisks on the lunar surface—which even popular astronomers such as Patrick Moore and Arthur C. Clarke have noted, but have declined to comment upon. David considers these obelisks to be the most conclusive evidence for the existence of extraterrestrials, but is resigned to the fact that such high profile scientists as Moore and Clarke don't dare to say as much for fear of losing their jobs and their credibility.

In addition, David has collected photographs of what appear to be pyramids and domed cities on the moon, indications of tunnels and bottomless craters on the lunar surface and even space bases on Mars.

"When I started my research I had no idea there were so many anomalies. Admittedly, some could have formed naturally, but there are too many which are perfectly symmetrical and geometrically aligned for them to be anything other than artificial. It's simply astounding. We cannot afford to ignore the facts any longer."

But whilst these "facts" certainly shake up our preconceptions, getting scientific institutions to accept that such anomalies are conclusive proof that the planets and moons of our solar system were inhabited in the past, and continue to be inhabited today, is strictly a non-starter.

"What I have discovered within our own solar system is quite contrary to what we have been told officially. For example, there are strong indications that there was once a planet between Mars and Jupiter where now there is only an asteroid belt. It may well be that one day science will discover that the debris of that asteroid belt is the remains of a once-fertile planet and that we are the alien visitors from that lost planet whom primitive man worshipped as gods. Modern man may be the extraterrestrial 'missing link' between Homo erectus and Homo sapiens.

"The simple fact is that while young people could take this all in at one go, the older generation, particularly those who have written the textbooks, couldn't handle a new reality. So government agencies seep the truth out a little at a time into the national psyche through 'unofficial' channels such as the whole New Age/esoteric underground network. NASA simply can't come right out and say what they've found, so they do what politicians do. They filter out information through controlled leaks to the mass media and in sugar-coated form in movies, TV series like *The X Files* and *Stargate*. Ideas that were once the exclusive preserve of 'eccentric' esoterics are now generally accepted thanks to the influence of *The X Files* and big budget Hollywood movies like *Close Encounters* and *Independence Day*."

Mass entertainment and popular culture may have planted the seeds of possibility, but the questions for the nuts and bolts sceptics remain: if there are so many UFOs out there with an interest in our planet, then how is it that comparatively few people have seen them? And how come military and government agencies are able to restrict public access to the facts?

"Good question. My belief differs from the others in one important respect. I say that for the extraterrestrials to have the kind of advanced technology that would enable them to travel such incredible distances they would have to have a corresponding level of consciousness, of understanding or spiritual maturity if you like, to have conceived of such a mission in the first place. They would understand that they couldn't interfere with other beings' lives, meddle with our development or manipulate us for their own ends because it would be karmically disastrous for all concerned. So instead they try to guide us towards a greater understanding of the universe by planting the idea in our minds of there being other forms of life through selected 'appearances.'

"You only have to look at the mass formation of UFOs sighted in broad daylight over Mexico City recently and captured on video. It was like they were saying, 'Hey, look at us! Take a picture!' They want us to see them and accept their existence as visitors, not as threats. Unfortunately a powerful element within the world's governments does not want us to fraternise with our new neighbours for obvious reasons."

David believes that it is not a question of whether the aliens are friendly or malevolent. He is convinced that it can't be as simple as that.

"I believe in a kind of *Star Trek* scenario with a federation of space-faring nations amongst whom are a rogue element or two on the fringes, just as there are belligerent nations on earth. I can't envisage them being either Messianic saviours or evil despots with plans for invasion. Taken as a whole they are undoubtedly good-natured, just as we are."

For non-believers the whole subject of UFOs has been confused by the CIA's recent admissions that some sightings can be attributed to top secret devices such as the Black Triangle spy probes whose existence the authorities had been denying for decades. David claims that these latest revelations only fan the flames of the smokescreen that has been put up by the authorities. The truth is more complex than either side of the UFO argument would have us believe.

In one of his earlier books, *Man Made UFOs 1944–1994*, which he co-authored with Renato Vesco, David reveals that a secret American saucer-shaped surveillance and strike craft project began when the Allies captured flying saucer technology from the Nazis at the end of World War II. But more startling still is the suggestion that around the same time they also uncovered a secret "saucer" base in South America established by followers of the eccentric Yugoslavian inventor Nicolas Tesla which the captured technicians claimed had already sent manned missions to Mars!

"Tesla was probably the greatest inventor who ever lived," says David who counts an indispensable biography of the man among his numerous titles.

> "And yet, few people have heard about him. He invented three-phased motors producing rotating magnetic fields decades before they were officially invented and were used to generate power for New York City. But the most remarkable aspect of Tesla's inventions is that they were not devised in the laboratory, but envisioned in Tesla's mind when he was an impoverished, uneducated teenager in Yugoslavia! It is my belief that he was reinventing devices from our ancient past."

According to David's exhaustive researches these ancient devices included aircraft. In *Vimana Aircraft of Ancient India and Atlantis* he provides lengthy and detailed descriptions of what he claims are ancient terrestrial aircraft taken from translations of Indian Sanskrit texts such as the *Ramayana*, *Mahabharata* and *Vimaanika Shastra* dating from 4,000 BCE. This he sees as evidence that the ancients had the technology for powered flight—namely mercury vortex propulsion. In fact, he describes the *Vimaanika Shastra* as "an entire flight manual," and in the *Mahabharata* the Indian gods are often depicted crossing the skies in "virmanas," a word which translates as "flying machine."

The following passage has often been quoted as an example of an ancient laser-like weapon, but it could equally apply to a volcanic eruption:

"A blazing missile possessed of the radiance of smokeless
fire was discharged. A thick gloom suddenly encom-
passed the hosts. All points of the compass were
enveloped in darkness. Evil-bearing winds began to
blow. Clouds roared into the higher air, showering
blood ... The world, scorched by the heat of that
weapon, seemed to be in a fever."

But if David's interpretation of these texts is correct and
we lost this archaic knowledge with the destruction of
advanced civilisations such as Atlantis, why did we not
pick up more or less where we left off with the help of the
survivors?

"That's another good question. My argument is that the
accepted view of human evolution as a steady progression
from darkness to light is wrong. If you consider European history and the development of what I'll call 'modern science,' you will see that there was a rollercoaster of
intellectual and spiritual illumination followed by periods of darkness and superstition. For example, it's well
known that the Greeks and Romans had an infinitely
superior knowledge of science and the earth than the
Europeans had later in the Dark Ages, when the Catholic
church suppressed so much of what was known to keep
the mass of the people in their place.

"My own studies of ancient texts and monuments
around the world and my esoteric researches clearly lead
to the revelation that human history, like life, is cyclical,
not linear. But the Western mind is so rigid that it cannot conceive of elder races having the insight and drive to
develop advanced technology. We are taught that our
ancestors were all primitives living in caves who, sud-

denly and inexplicably, woke up one morning about 200,000 years ago and decided to build incredible monuments like the pyramids. It makes no sense and archaeologists readily admit that they have no explanation for it, but nevertheless they refuse to believe anything other than this traditional, accepted viewpoint.

"Every year we make new discoveries and are forced to push back the age when man started to behave like an intelligent being, so perhaps one day mainstream science will acknowledge that our oversimplified, arrogant view of history needs to be rewritten."

If the truth is out there, then, in my opinion, David is the man most likely to find it.

6

THE SIRIUS CONNECTION

THE PEOPLE OF the Dogon tribe of Mali, West Africa, appear to possess a detailed and accurate knowledge of the universe which they claim was entrusted to their ancestors by visitors from the stars. The tribe have known for centuries that the dog star Sirius, the brightest star in the night sky, is actually a double star—a fact that was not known to astronomers until 1862. The star's companion, Sirius B, had been invisible to even the most powerful telescopes until the American astronomer Alvan Graham Clark discovered it quite by chance. More remarkable is the fact that the Dogon describe Sirius B as being of denser matter than Sirius and state that it has a 50-year elliptical orbit. Both facts were only confirmed in the 1920s when the irregular motion of Sirius was explained by the discovery that Sirius B was a "white dwarf" whose superdensity could exert a gravitational force strong enough to influence the orbit of the larger star. One might expect an uneducated people to depict Sirius in the centre of the smaller star's orbit, but again, the Dogon position it correctly in their sand drawings and cave paintings—at the edge of the ellipse.

Dogon tradition records that knowledge of Sirius B and other astronomical data (such as the fact that the planets in our solar system revolve around the sun, that the moon is dry and lifeless and that the earth spins on its axis had been entrusted to their ancestors by fish-like gods from a third star in the Sirius system almost 5,000 years ago. (Confirmation of the existence of this third star did not come until 1995 adding another remarkable facet to the Sirius–Dogon mystery.)

The Dogon called these gods the Nommo and incorporated stories about them in their rites and rituals as well as in their carvings, architecture, paintings and ceremonial costumes. They describe the Nommo as "the monitors of the universe," "guardians of its spiritual principles" and, "masters of the water" who arrived on earth in an ark. Their detailed description of the ark and its descent sounds remarkably like a rocket-powered spacecraft which is said to have cast down its "word" in four directions, whipping up a small sandstorm and leaving marks on impact.

The landing is said to have taken place in a region to the north-east of their present settlement on the Bandiagara Plateau, in an area bordering Egypt from where their ancestors originated.

However, other cultures in the region, and further afield, appear to mirror the Dogon legends which suggests that either the Dogon's ancestors assimilated these tales from their neighbours, or that there were indeed landings by extraterrestrials to which various ancient civilisations were witness.

In Greek mythology the island of Rhodes is said to have

been civilised by dog-headed amphibious aliens called Telchines whom the Greek historian Diodorus Siculus described as "the discoverers of certain arts and other things which are useful for the life of mankind." Similarly, the Babylonian priest Berossus wrote of the Annedoti, fish-like creatures who emerged from a great egg to "humanise mankind" under the directions of a leader named Oannes, a name strikingly similar to the Mayan word "oaana," meaning "he who has residence in water."

A RATIONAL EXPLANATION?

IT IS POSSIBLE that the Egyptians rather than extraterrestrials were the source of Dogon knowledge for they shared the belief in the significance of Sirius whose heliacal rising mirrored the contours of the Nile. It was for this reason, and the fact that Sirius is the brightest star in the night sky, that the Egyptians identified it with the goddess Isis. Perhaps the Egyptians also knew of the existence of Sirius B, as is suggested by the fact that in Egyptian mythology Isis is given a shadowy companion, the dog god Anubis.

Another possibility is that the Dogon's astronomical knowledge may have originated in more recent times from Western missionaries, students at the Moslem University in nearby Timbuktu or from French schools in the region, but this can be dismissed by the antiquity of the carvings and paintings. Moreover, the tribal priests were evidently reluctant to disclose these secrets which they held to be sacred and it seems highly unlikely that they would have regarded them as such had they originated from itinerant travellers or academics. It was only when two eminent

French anthropologists, Marcel Griaule and Germaine Dieterlen, gained the tribe's trust by living with them almost continually for over 20 years from 1931 that the priests proved willing to share their secrets.

Griaule and Dieterlen published their findings in an obscure academic journal in 1950, but it wasn't until 1976 that the Sirius connection became common knowledge following the publication of *The Sirius Mystery* by Robert Temple.

Temple is a highly respected classical scholar and Fellow of the Royal Astronomical Society who readily admits that there are still many unanswerable questions about which he can only speculate, but he remains convinced that there were a number of roughly simultaneous landings by a technically advanced race of extraterrestrials in ancient Egypt and Sumeria around 3,500 BCE. He also believes that these visitors helped our distant ancestors to establish the first civilisations.

But how was he able to deduce that there may have been extraterrestrial contact in antiquity from the myths of ancient Sumeria, Egypt and West Africa?

"The large amount of highly specific numerical data and astronomical information which these cultures had preserved convinced me that I wasn't simply dealing with pseudo-religious mythology. I was able to prove much of it to be astrophysically correct. For example, they had recorded exact orbital periods of certain stars and planets and were able to describe the nature of what we now call superdense matter."

Temple is keen to clear up the popular misconception that

he might be suggesting a direct contact between the Dogon and extraterrestrials.

> "As far as I know, extraterrestrials did not come to Mali. The Dogon are not claiming alien contact and I haven't suggested any. What I am suggesting is that their very distant ancestors in Babylon, Sumeria and Egypt appear to have had contact around 3,500 BCE. The connection with the Dogon comes about through separate independent studies by various anthropologists who have traced the Dogon line back to these ancient civilisations. The most convincing evidence of a link, as far as I am concerned, is the use of shared vocabulary, particularly of sacred names. For example, the Babylonians called their sacred mountain, where the sun rose each morning, Mashu. I have proved Mashu to be an imported word which derives from the ancient Egyptian word for 'behold, the sun.' The connection is so obvious it's painful."

One crucial question remains though: how were highly advanced ideas regarding the nature of space, matter and the planets conveyed by the visitors to our comparatively primitive ancestors assuming they did not share a common language?

> "That's quite a question. We have no idea how they put across these concepts or how they taught our ancestors what they felt they needed to know for their development. What we do know is that the beings who claimed to have come from Sirius were aquatic or amphibious. We don't know if they breathed earth's atmosphere or were equipped with air tanks like deep-sea divers. We

can't possibly know their true nature at this distance in time, but we do know about their physical appearance because it is described very clearly in ancient texts and in word-of-mouth traditions. I have not the slightest doubt that we are talking about physical beings rather than spirit entities seen in visions, because of the descriptions of their appearance and actions which were recorded by our ancestors. You only have to examine the profusion of detail regarding the spacecraft to appreciate that. The Dogon tradition clearly distinguishes between the orbiting base, or mother ship, and the landing vehicles, which is pretty sophisticated of them. The Dogon say that when the Nommos came, the first thing their ancestors saw was a new star which I believe was the orbiting base. They describe it as contracting and expanding. Then from it came another craft which they describe as an ark which descended with a mighty roar in dust and fire—just the effect we would expect from a rocket-powered craft.

"The tradition is that the Nommos taught man civilising principles such as law and the cultivation of grain, but they hedged their bets by establishing centres in both Egypt and Sumeria in case one failed.

"I believe it is significant that both centres were established near water because both the Sumerians and the Egyptians talk of the visitors as having fish-like extremities. In fact the Babylonians, descendants of the Sumerians, remark that their gods retired each night to the water."

In the 20 years since the original publication of *The Sirius Mystery*, Temple's conviction that there was extraterrestrial contact in antiquity has deepened as he has uncovered uncannily similar descriptions of fish-like gods as the founders of civilisation in the myths of other cultures, namely Chinese and Greek. But he refuses to be tempted into speculating whether or not the visitors entrusted the ancients with advanced technical knowledge which was then lost with the decline of their civilisations.

"Why are people so eager to believe that extraterrestrials would hand over high technological know-how to our comparatively primitive ancestors? Why would an advanced species give computers to a cultured, but otherwise near-primitive society? I consider that they gave us a great deal. They set up the first civilisations and introduced us to the principles of agriculture and law etc., which to me is a greater gift than if they had dropped a cure for cancer in our ancestors' laps. It's puerile and stupid to think of ancient extraterrestrial contact as some sort of intergalactic aid mission. Extraterrestrials are not in the business of stopping life from running its natural evolutionary course or of acting as supernatural beings with a spiritual mission to bring enlightenment to the heathens. But somehow it seems they had learnt that we were at an early stage in our development and could do with being introduced to the higher principles of civilisation. Or perhaps they didn't know what stage we were at until they arrived here. We can't possibly know. But I am sure of my research. I have never started out with any preconceptions, nor have I ever set out to prove a pet theory and selected the evidence to fit it. I have never insisted upon being right."

SPECULATIONS ON THE SPHINX

RECENTLY TEMPLE HAS challenged both traditionalists and revisionists on the subject of the origin and purpose of that most enigmatic of ancient monuments, the Sphinx. He energetically disputes the claims made by maverick Egyptologist John West (see page 25) that the Sphinx was carved in the image of a lion:

> "It amazes me that so many people blindly accept one man's conclusion that the Sphinx may have originally had the body and head of a lion while their own eyes would surely tell them that it has no leonine characteristics at all! Even allowing for the refurbishments carried out under the orders of Pharaoh Kafre in 2,500 BCE there is no trace at all of leonine features. There is no lion's tail with the tuft, no lion-like haunches or trace of where a mane might have been. Most significantly it has a perfectly straight back which is uncharacteristic of a lion, but is perfectly consistent with the body of a dog. It is my contention that the Sphinx was originally a crouching Anubis—the jackal-headed God of the Dead, the son of Osiris and companion of the goddess Isis. That ties in too with the idea that the three pyramids were erected by extraterrestrials to accurately represent the alignment of their home planetary system of Sirius.
>
> > "It is generally accepted that the three pyramids were part of an Anubis cult and so it is more than likely that the Sphinx would have taken the form of Anubis as the guardian of that sacred site."

If it is true that we had contact with an advanced extraterrestrial race in antiquity why is their influence so faint now? Why is modern man so reluctant to accept the existence of a greater reality and why are other races so reluctant to make contact with us again?

> "That raises a serious question about the nature of our species. We only have to remind ourselves that in these so-called enlightened times we have had two world wars and millions of murders by so-called civilised people. Perhaps no major extraterrestrial contact has been made because we are considered by other races to be a psychopathic species and they have put us in a kind of cosmic quarantine. We might be an aberration, not them."

RETURN OF THE GODS?

"I'm very hopeful of a return visit by those who came in ancient times. The extraterrestrials must have mastered suspended animation as a fundamental element of interstellar travel. It is also highly unlikely that they would have planned their visit to earth as a one-off trip. So I envisage them still out there orbiting in suspended animation—the very same personalities who came to the ancient Egyptians and Sumerians—awaiting their wakeup call from some kind of super-computer which would have been monitoring our progress and recording the new languages which our visitors will have to master.

"My hopes are pinned on the fact that the Dogon say the new star left the sky when the visitors departed and became what they called the Star of the Tenth Moon. All the cultures that I have studied say the visitors retreated to the outer regions of the solar system. If you think this through it can only point to Phoebe, one of Saturn's moons. Phoebe is the only one of Saturn's moons which appears to be perfectly round and smooth—like an artificial structure rather than a planetary body. This was confirmed for me by a NASA scientist. Phoebe also has a wildly retrograde orbit and is the tenth-largest of Saturn's moons. Some of the others are no more than rocks or space garbage. So Phoebe could literally be the Star of the Tenth Moon."

It would appear then the only thing we have to fear is not the visitors themselves but our reaction to them. After all, Temple's research suggests they are founders of high civilisation. He explains:

"They have a lot of stock invested in our planet and they went to infinite pains to get us going along the right lines, so it is inconceivable that they will destroy their 'experiment.' But then again, they were helpful on their terms. What we might consider to be progress they might see as destruction. Being amphibious they won't be happy to find our oceans and rivers as polluted as we have made them. And, of course, we are a lot more dangerous now than we were in 3,500 BCE. Who knows what they will do if our first reaction is to fire atomic rockets or ground-to-space lasers at them!"

7

ANCIENT ASTRONAUTS AND THE NAZCA ENIGMA

BETWEEN THE ANDES and the coast of Peru lies a vast arid region of 500 square miles known as the Nazca plateau. Aside from the odd crop of hills it appears to be a barren, featureless place, and yet etched into the earth are to be found huge figures of birds, insects and elaborate abstract patterns dating back some 1,500 years. The scale and anatomical accuracy of the drawings, some of which stretch up to 5 miles across, are astonishing in themselves, but the most remarkable and inexplicable aspect is the fact they can only be seen and appreciated as complete pictures from the air.

A number of elaborate theories have been produced to explain how a primitive people could have made such elaborate drawings and why they should have designed them to be seen to best advantage from the sky. The most implausible of these states that the lines indicate a landing

site for extraterrestrial spacecraft whose occupants had
come to earth in prehistoric times (between 10,000 and
40,000 years ago) to accelerate human evolution through
genetic engineering. Proponents of this theory ask us to
believe that these superior beings, who it is claimed mated
with early man to produce Homo sapiens, were the true
architects of the pyramids and other monuments of the
ancient world and were later worshipped and mythologised as gods by our ancestors.

Such theories surfaced periodically in the 1950s and
60s on the fringes of the academic world only to be dismissed by the scientific establishment as ludicrous, but in
1970 a Swiss hotelier-turned-writer brought them to the
attention of the general public in a series of books which
became instant bestsellers.

Erich Von Daniken shared the same approach to the
subject of extraterrestrial intervention as many writers on
the esoteric with a pet theory to prove. In *Chariots of the
Gods* and its sequels, *Return to the Stars* and *Gold of the
Gods*, Von Daniken appeared to have set out to prove a
preconceived idea which evidently appealed to his vivid
imagination, fashioning the facts to fit the theory and
allegedly overlooking any which did not conform, or
which he considered to be inconvenient.

In addition to stating that the Nazca lines had been built
by "unknown intelligences" as an "improvised airfield for
their spacecraft" he also credited the aliens with having
constructed such marvels of ancient engineering as the
Gateway of the Sun at Tiahuanaco, Bolivia, the megalithic
walls at Ollantaytambo, Peru, and the Sphinx and pyramids of ancient Egypt. But as far as the Nazca "airfield"
enigma is concerned, the respected German scientist Maria
Reiche, who has studied the lines on site for more than 50

years, dismissed Von Daniken's conclusion by pointing out that the ground was far too soft for a craft of any kind to land and take off. "The spacemen would have gotten stuck," she wryly remarked.

It now seems likely that the drawings had originally been plotted on a small scale and then squared up to full size by the indigenous people. Their purpose, according to Johan Reinhard, an expert in Andean mythology, was to appease the gods who, the people believed, would marvel at their splendour from the sky and reward them with the vital rainwater needed for survival.

Having erected or inspired every impressive monument of the ancient world, Von Daniken would have us believe that the gods departed leaving a trail of ancient artefacts such as the "dry cell batteries" and crystal lenses found in Mesopotamia, the astronomical "calculator" of Antikythera and a host of stone carvings and cave paintings representing aerials, astronauts, rockets and even primitive heart-transplant operations.

The generally accepted view that the winged gods depicted in cave paintings and sculpted in stone are more likely to be characters of religious or mystical significance does not seem to have occurred to him. Nor does the fact that ancient architects had a grasp of hydrodynamics and other basic engineering principles involving pulleys and levers, which enabled them to transport and erect the massive stone blocks from which their impressive monuments were made.

Von Daniken's spurious speculations naturally infuriated serious archaeologists, historians and theologians alike who condemned him for drawing erroneous, preconceived conclusions from very dubious "evidence," for propagating a host of factual errors and for claiming to have conducted research on sites which it is alleged he never visited.

The most notorious incident was that in which he claimed to have unearthed a treasure trove of prehistoric artefacts, including a library of metal plates inscribed with the record of an alien landing, in a secret system of tunnels in Ecuador. However, his guide later denied that they had entered the caves in question which were blocked by fallen rubble and claimed that Von Daniken resorted to photographing relics in the local museum which were mostly "junk." However, Von Daniken stubbornly and emphatically refuses to admit any deceit or failing on his part:

> "It is not true that I have admitted to saying that I was not at certain sites that I wrote about. That is all part of an old misunderstanding which stems from an interview with the German magazine *Der Spiegel* 20 years ago in which we were talking about one of my earliest books, *The Gold of the Gods*, where I mention an underground cave in Ecuador. Now, from the beginning I clearly admitted that I was not in the main entrance to the cave—in fact, I was at a side entrance—but it was taken as being an admission that I wasn't there at all! Maybe it was my own fault. In those days I didn't take enough care about how I phrased my answers when talking to journalists. And I was concerned with a promise I had made to the person who discovered the cave not to reveal the fact that it had a main entrance for fear of inviting treasure hunters and tourists."

Von Daniken also categorically denies any accusations of wilfully inventing details to support his theories:

"I have always been very conscientious in my research. At the back of all my books I have detailed my sources and listed precisely where my facts and quotations come from, as they do in scientific literature—even though my books are not scientific, but popular books. Still, it is not only unfair of my critics to claim that I am careless in my research, it is hurtful to be personally attacked in this way."

Despite Von Daniken's assertion that he conscientiously quotes his sources on specific points, the writer Colin Wilson, for one, has accused him of failing to acknowledge the work of early "interventionist" writers such as Jacques Bergier and Louis Pauwels from whose work Von Daniken is said to have borrowed wholesale. Von Daniken's defence appears to be that it was wrong of the world's press to damn both him and his whole concept of extraterrestrial intervention merely because he might have been "careless" with a few facts. It is clear that he still feels ill-used and misrepresented by the media, particularly the English press.

"Only the other month an English paper made a big story around the latest theory of two British scientists who claim to have finally proven the origin and purpose of the Nazca lines. The paper made a big fanfare about the lines being connected with a water cult and ran the story with a big screaming headline which said 'Von Daniken Finally Disproved!' I could almost have laughed because I published a book in Germany whose title translates as *Science for Eternity* which deals with Nazca exclusively. It includes all the theories connected with the lines including the idea that they were to do with a water cult which is, in fact, an old idea and still not conclusively proven to my satisfaction. Of course that sort of story gets picked up by the press in Europe and then I have to defend myself over here all over again.

"The problem is that although I have written 22 books, the last eight were not published on the English market, so my arguments have not been presented coherently. All of my books have been translated into other languages and so I've been able to argue my case, and defend myself and my claims in person in interviews, but not in England where only my critics' voices are heard."

However, it may well be that the essence of his theory, if not the details, is one day proved to be correct; that we owe a leap in consciousness and our physical evolution to the influence of a more advanced civilisation from another planet. We still have no plausible explanation for such fantastic structures as the ruins of Nan Madol in the South Pacific where over 400,000 basalt pillars lie scattered on the jungle floor, each up to 40 feet long and weighing over 10 tonnes, and the feats of ancient engineering in Iraq and Peru, to name but a few. However, in attributing every inexplicable marvel of the ancient world to external forces Von Daniken, and those who subscribe to the ancient astronaut theory, commit one cardinal error. They undermine the ingenuity, achievements and aspirations of our ancestors, aspirations which enabled them to leave the security of the caves and set a course for the stars.

THE SCEPTICAL SCHOLAR

EMMET SWEENY, THE eminent expert in biblical archaeology and author of *The Genesis of Israel and Egypt*, responded to my interview with Von Daniken by debunking the ancient astronaut theory entirely:

> "Nothing of what he {Von Daniken} says has any foundation in fact and cannot be substantiated by the evidence in any way whatsoever. The idea that the high civilisations of the past could not have been created by human beings, and therefore must have been created by aliens is a supposition which is completely untenable."

Sweeny concedes that ancient mythologies do appear to record incredible events, but these events are open to a number of interpretations which are far less fanciful than those proposed by Von Daniken and his devotees.

> "Ancient people did believe that the gods dwelt in the heavens, but the fact is that ancient mythology quite clearly tells us that the ancient people regarded the planets themselves as gods. Mars, for example, was the God Mars. It didn't just represent him ... [Nor is there] a need to postulate aliens from outer space in order to explain something which is actually a common archetype amongst visionaries and mystics."

Sweeny states that he has found no evidence of extraterrestrial intervention in ancient times and claims that our evolution and the development of civilisation can be easily traced along lines that are logical and consistent with a gradually awakening consciousness. He is adamant that the Egyptian pyramids and other wonders of the ancient world were man-made, and that it has been possible to engineer the alien component into the equation simply because of chronological inconsistencies perpetuated by the academic establishment. He points out that the establishment view is that the pyramids were built in the 3rd millennium BCE with copper tools which Von Daniken and his followers have rightly seized upon as being implausible and impractical given the scale of the structures. Sweeny instead suggests that they were erected much later and cites the chronicles of the Greek writer Herodotus who says that they were built before the Ethiopian invasion in the 8th century BCE when the Egyptians would have access to iron and steel tools. Sweeny accuses the academics of ignoring Herodotus and other ancient sources on the basis that because they are ancient they are not reliable, and then of turning a blind eye to the discovery of iron artefacts in pyramid period burials because they do not fit in with the accepted theory.

If Sweeny is right and the pyramids date from 800 BCE this would also explain how the ancient architects were able to incorporate a high degree of accuracy into their construction as they would have been able to utilise the principles of Pythagorean geometry.

There is no record of these structures having been erected by gods, but there are records which state that they were built in honour of the gods.

"The idea that the gods are up there in the sky is the most primeval and universal of human ideas and it has a very clear and simple explanation," says Sweeney.

He cites the controversial theory of Dr. Emmanuel Velikovsky, a one-time partner of Albert Einstein, who argued that many of the world's most enduring myths, specifically the legends of lost continents and the Great Flood, originated with a series of real natural catastrophes in the 2nd millennium BCE. A collision with a comet is thought to have altered the earth's axis, whipping up colossal tidal waves which flooded the continents, creating extensive tectonic plate activity which threw up new mountain ranges and sent islands to the bottom of the sea. It was therefore natural for our ancestors to look to the skies not only as the source of their sustenance, as symbolised by the sun, but also as the source of the gods' wrath and displeasure.

According to Sweeny, many ancient cultures used meteorites in ritual purposes because they saw them as coming from heaven, and for that reason impact sites, such as Stonehenge, became sacred ceremonial places.

> "All over Western Europe stone circles have been found to contain traces of radioactivity and that, again, can be well explained by the fact that they almost certainly were erected on a meteorite impact site ... All the most sacred relics of the ancients were meteorites and they were revered simply because they had come from the sky which was the home of the gods."

Sweeny concedes that Von Daniken's ideas have struck a chord because they have an element of truth, but believes the mysteries of the universe are not to be solved by looking to the skies, but rather to the ideas which lie behind ancient belief systems which gave life its meaning.

8

THE STARGATE CONSPIRACY

LYNN PICKNETT AND Clive Prince, authors of *The Stargate Conspiracy*, claim to have identified a fundamental flaw in the orthodox world view of academics and archaeologists which states that the ancient Egyptians built the pyramids for burial purposes using engineering skills that were lost with the decline of their civilisation.

> PICKNETT: "One of the things that impressed me most when I visited the tombs in the Valley of the Kings was the wealth of inscriptions which cover the walls, the sarcophagi, in fact, every inch of the interior. But there are none in the pyramids at Giza. If the Giza pyramids had been built as tombs for the dead pharaoh surely they would have been ornamented in the same way with the spells that were intended to assist the soul's journey through the afterlife."

Picknett and Prince suggest that their efforts to expose an

alleged conspiracy by "alternative" historians and government intelligence agencies to create what they call a "hybrid fundamentalism" is more important than the question of whether or not humanity was once aided by extraterrestrials with their own agenda.

PICKNETT: "If our theory is correct then the intelligence agencies have been manipulating the public in the same way that the Nazi propaganda machine 're-educated' the German population to support the war and its programme of genocide. Intelligence agencies know that if the public can be 'encouraged' to focus its latent fears and insecurities on an alien race, imagined or otherwise, then it will be far easier to control.

"But while the ancient astronaut theory cannot be conclusively dismissed, it is ultimately negative because it undermines our self-esteem. I don't personally feel that the unsolved mysteries of the pyramids are as crucial to our understanding of human history as many make them out to be. My feeling is that humans did build them, and that the other impressive monuments of the ancient world were also man-made, but I'm uncomfortable with the assumption that this means they had superior knowledge and technology gained from extraterrestrials.

"What we do know for a fact is that the ancient Egyptians had an impressive knowledge of astronomy and chemistry which the academic establishment appears to be very reluctant to acknowledge. It suits the scholars to believe that our ancestors were superstitious primitives, although archaeological and documentary evidence contradicts this somewhat arrogant complacency.

"There were some very basic principles, such as arch and bridge building, that ancient Egyptian architects clearly didn't know, which they would have done if they had had extraterrestrial assistance. It is really too big an assumption to make that civilisation had to be kick-started on the road to progress by aliens whose language we wouldn't have even understood—never mind their advanced mathematics—simply because we can't figure out how they made such accurate measurements or moved those massive stone blocks."

Picknett and Prince are particularly critical of the new wave of revisionist historians, such as Graham Hancock and Robert Bauval, who have speculated that the wonders of the ancient world are either the work of survivors from a lost continent or were overseen by a superior intelligence from space.

PRINCE: "Hancock appears to present a very convincing case for a shared heritage, but if you examine his findings closely they are very selective and fail to offer anything that could be called concrete or conclusive. In one of his earlier books, *Fingerprints of the Gods*, he catalogues a number of amazing artefacts which defy a traditional explanation by orthodox archaeologists, but he doesn't have anything to back up his own theories as to their origin. Writers such as Hancock often come up with some incredible artefacts, but they insist on imposing their own ideas on them, or they try to make them fit with something else found elsewhere in the world which is unrelated. This 'pick and mix' approach is ultimately self-defeating as it only succeeds in shrouding the thing in even more mystery.

"A classic example of this is when he dates the Sphinx to a supposed tropical period in Egypt's prehistoric past. But when we double-checked the data we found no evidence for a wet period in the 11th millennium, in fact quite the contrary. Dr. Sarah O'Mara of Drylands Research at Sheffield University, a world authority on desert climates, has stated that before 8,000 BCE there is no evidence that humans were living in the region as it was too dry and cold for habitation. We have no argument with Dr. Robert Schoch's assertion that the Sphinx could be as old as 6,500 BCE, but anything beyond that seems to be wishful thinking on the part of Hancock who needs it to date from 10,500 BCE to fit his Atlantean scenario."

Picknett and Prince contend that the ancient astronaut theory is weak as it depends upon a literal interpretation of mythology where the gods of old are understood to be visitors from space.

PRINCE: "We don't have any logical objections to extraterrestrial contact or a migration of survivors from a lost civilisation. In fact, we admit that there is a convincing argument to be made for both, but what we do object to is the approach of writers like Erich Von Daniken and Zecharia Sitchin who interpret every myth literally as a matter of course without considering that it may be symbolic of a spiritual experience or have been created to convey a moral or eternal truth, which is surely the primary purpose of these tales.

"The problem is that these New Age myths are self-creating and self-perpetuating. By that I mean that someone who is a devotee of Edgar Cayce, for example, and who believes that beneath the Sphinx is a secret library of

Atlantean wisdom, will do his or her utmost to convince others of its existence. Even when they find that it does not exist they will continue to speculate on its location. Eventually it will become clear that they have led everyone up a blind alley, just as the leaders of apocalyptic cults often do, but they can spin this search out over a very long time and disseminate their own beliefs in the process.

"In the autumn of 1999 Dr. Joseph Schor, who heads an organisation dedicated to finding evidence of Atlantis, was given a licence to search for the Hall of Records beneath the Sphinx. Now other investigators will be able to claim that the Egyptian authorities officially recognised the existence of the Atlantean archives because it is listed on the licence, even though they simply recorded what he said he was looking for. That's how these myths manage to take on a veneer of fact. Personally, I don't believe that there is anything of value remaining to be discovered at these sites. They have all been thoroughly searched and documented. Does anyone really believe that trained archaeologists could have overlooked such an important find?"

As much as one might like to believe that our ancestors had contact with benign beings from another world—if only to feel that we are not alone in the universe—Picknett and Prince have reason to be rational and realistic. One only has to be reminded of the excitement whipped up by the Face On Mars fiasco to feel that a healthy dose of scepticism would not be amiss until all the facts are before us.

A photo of the Cydonia region of Mars taken by NASA's Viking Orbiter in 1976 showed what appeared to be a sculpted face on the planet's surface. Many people believed that it was the remains of a Martian sphinx surrounded by pyramids and that the architects had come to earth in ancient times to help the Egyptians build similar structures.

Over the next 20 years a number of prominent scientists and celebrity experts such as Arthur C. Clarke were persuaded to join in an orchestrated campaign to pressure NASA into blanketing the area with high resolution images to dispel the suspicion that the U.S. space agency was concealing its findings from the public. A veritable industry of sensationalistic literature and TV documentaries turned the screw on the conspiracy theory, fuelled by the sudden failure of the onboard computers during the August 1993 survey at the very moment that it was programmed to make passes over the planet's surface. This untimely and costly failure certainly looked suspicious and the case for the face lobby made the most of it, but then in April 1998 the Global Explorer took razor sharp pictures of the region and NASA released them immediately. After all the speculation and hype the face was finally and conclusively revealed to be a cluster of craters and mountains. The features of the face could still be seen, but the curious effect produced by the shadows had vanished in the light. Not surprisingly perhaps, the most ardent and vociferous campaigners for the face resorted to computer enhancement to "restore" the illusion and return to the fray.

PRINCE: "This preoccupation with lost civilisations and alien artefacts reveals that what we have really lost is the sense of self-confidence with which the Egyptians built the pyramids. They believed in themselves because they believed in the immortality of the soul; that they were each a spark of the divine. Those men and women who made great scientific achievements in our time such as

Einstein did so because they too believed in themselves. But we have lost the belief in our own infinite potential and with it the vision which inspired the ancients to build their empires. If you doubt it you only have to look to the media to see how passive we have become under the deluge of information overload. I recently heard a caller to a radio station claim that everything invented after World War II was the direct result of technology recovered from the Roswell crash! I find that sad and rather disturbing."

PICKNETT: "The important point to stress is what these revisionist histories tell us about the human condition. They reveal that we are willing to hand over our heritage and deny the achievements that humanity has made because we have been conditioned from childhood to undervalue ourselves. For 2,000 years we have been taught that we have no divine spark, that we are miserable sinners unworthy of divine love unless we earn it, so we aspire to attention and even affection of a sort from anywhere 'up there' in the heavens. All we are saying is, for goodness' sake, let's start behaving like gods again."

9

THE LIVING PLANET

SCIENCE HAS SUCCEEDED in demystifying many of the enigmas of the natural world, but even the greatest minds admit that they are unable to explain why life continues to flourish on earth contrary to the laws of physics.

Our rivers should be saturated in salt from aeons of water erosion and yet, something appears to have regulated the fresh water eco system so that life can be sustained. And after a century of being choked with industrial pollutants, fossil fuels and exhaust fumes, the atmosphere should contain enough carbon dioxide to kill every person on the planet, according to the principles of thermodynamics. Whilst matter and energy obey the laws of science, the earth itself appears to be exerting its own influence in order to ensure our survival.

THE EARTH GODDESS

THE IDEA THAT the earth is a living entity which nurtures all life, as a mother nurtures her children, was a central belief of primitive man. Prehistoric people and the pagans of later centuries envisaged the earth as a goddess to be worshipped and appeased, in return for which she would bless the faithful with fertility and bountiful harvests. The ancient Greeks called her Gaia, a name borrowed by the British scientist James Lovelock in his book *Gaia: The Practical Science of Planetary Medicine*.

Lovelock formulated his controversial theory of the earth as a living entity in the 1960s. Whilst Lovelock and his assistant, biologist Lynn Margulis, did not subscribe to the belief that the earth is a conscious, sentient being they were able to present a convincing case for it being more than a mass of inanimate rock which fate has randomly favoured with life. This had been the accepted scientific view for more than a century. Lovelock and Margulis turned this cherished theory on its head when they suggested that our planet is a self-regulating, self-sustaining physiological organism capable of influencing the chemical composition and temperature of the four physical realms—the atmosphere, biosphere, lithosphere and hydrosphere. Furthermore, they claimed that the ability of the earth to heal itself suggests that it purges itself of pollutants in the same way as our bodies fight infection which is, again, contrary to the orthodox scientific view.

ENERGY PATTERNS AND SACRED SITES

IF THE EARTH is a living organism it is reasonable to assume that it will radiate some form of energy. Psychics are believed to be able to "see" the aura of etheric (vital) energy surrounding living beings and mystics have spoken of the vibrancy of nature, but no one has yet measured or in any way proven the existence of earth energy. However, attempts have been made to trace the lines of this invisible force by the unscientific but unerringly accurate method known as dowsing, either with a pendulum or divining rod, to reveal the relationship between the lines and significant sacred sites of the ancient world.

In the 1940s a provincial English solicitor and amateur dowser, Guy Underwood, claimed to have confirmed the existence of underground streams at several sites which had earlier been officially identified by members of the British Museum. Underwood's divining rod had pulled to the left to indicate the course of the water as he had expected, leaving him with a set of parallel lines between 1 and 2 feet apart that marked the width of the underground stream. But in a second series of readings he found himself being led to the right as the rod traced a series of complex geometric patterns which appeared to indicate the existence of lines of force under the earth. Underwood suspected that our ancestors were sensitive to these invisible forces and that they had erected their sacred monuments where concentrations of what he dubbed "geodetic force" had been divined.

Encouraged by his findings Underwood made a survey of Stonehenge and other sacred sites, including the famous giant chalk figures carved into the hillsides at Wandlebury, Uffington and Cerne Abbas. At each of these he discovered that their boundaries and features conformed to the lines of geodetic force that he was able to trace with his divining rod. He concluded that the philosophers and priests of the old religions seemed to have believed that, particularly when manifested in spiral forms, the earth force was involved with the generative powers of nature, and kept all nature in equilibrium.

Of course it is possible that Underwood unconsciously influenced the pull of the rod, but that would not invalidate his findings as the rod is believed to act like an antenna for the psychic sensitivity of the dowser. The distinguished British academic and archaeologist Professor Tom Lethbridge, for example, maintained that the divining rod acted as an extension of the archaeologist's intuition, having proven its potential for himself during an archaeological expedition when he successfully located veins of volcanic rock far underground on Lundy Island. There is a wealth of anecdotal evidence of a similar nature attesting to the power of the pendulum, but whilst evidence of that nature can be impressive it is not conclusive proof. However, anyone who has seen a dowser in action, or who has felt the pull of the rod or pendulum for themselves will find it difficult to deny that there is something in it.

It is possible that the earth generates geodetic force in a similar way in which the human body radiates its vital force. These ripples could exert a subtle influence on the nerve cells of all living things which share the same vibration, although each of us is probably sensitive to it to different degrees. That might explain why we can be uplifted by the atmosphere of certain locations and depressed by others, even if there has not been a violent incident at the site. These might be places of negative or positive polarity.

The belief in the existence of an invisible matrix of

energy beneath the earth is not confined to modern eso-
tericists or independently minded academics. It was central
to the beliefs and practices of the ancient Chinese who
believed that the earth's current was the expression of primal negative and positive forces. They sought to channel
this energy by erecting pagodas where they thought the
current may be blocked by topographical features, a principle which is central to the practice of acupuncture in
which needles are inserted at blocked energy points. Here
the human body is seen as an expression of the natural
world.

SACRED STONES

IN RECENT YEARS the many sacred stone circles scattered across Europe have come under the scrutiny of scientists and academics who suspect that our pagan
ancestors might have erected these ancient sites to serve as
a focus for a natural, rather than a supernatural force. Prior
to the 1930s the accepted view was that sites such as
Stonehenge had been built by primitive people as temples
to an anonymous deity to whom they sacrificed unwilling
victims. However, in 1934, a Scottish engineer, Alexander
Thom, revealed what he believed to be the true purpose of
such sites and in doing so upset the conventional image of
pre-Christian Europe as having been inhabited by ignorant,
superstitious savages.

Thom discovered that a line of stones, or menhirs, leading to a megalithic stone circle overlooking Loch Roag in
the Outer Hebrides was in perfect alignment with the pole
star. However, at the time that these monoliths were
erected, in the 5th century BCE, the celestial pattern would

have been entirely different, meaning that the stones could not have been erected using the pole star as a marker. If the stars were not their guide, the architects of this and other ancient sites must have had a rudimentary knowledge of geometry and basic engineering skills to have placed the stones in their pattern with such accuracy.

Thom evidently found the idea as incredible as his colleagues, to whom he initially presented his findings, and so to substantiate his theory he devoted the rest of his life to visiting various prehistoric sites across Europe where he took detailed measurements. His dedication was rewarded with the staggering discovery that each and every site shared a standard unit of measurement, which Thom called the megalithic yard (2.72 feet). If the people of prehistoric Europe had shared a common knowledge of geometry and engineering which enabled them to erect sacred circles with considerable skill and accuracy, the sites must have served a significant purpose. But why would they go to such trouble if the purpose of the sites had been merely to appease their gods? Surely a rough stone altar would have sufficed. Thom compared his calculations from the various sites and was staggered to discover that the positions of the stones in each and every one of them could have been used for predicting eclipses of the sun and moon.

His conclusions, published as *Megalithic Lunar Observatories*, were elaborated upon in the 1960s by a British Professor, Gerald Hawkins, who was able to explain the purpose of several curious features at Stonehenge which had puzzled archaeologists for decades. Hawkins computer-generated a celestial map of the region as it would have appeared in the 2nd millennium and found that a lunar or solar eclipse occurred every 18.61 years when the winter moon was dissected by the Heel Stone.

To predict a series of eclipses, all the ancients had to do would be to calculate the interval between the eclipses. An eclipse of the moon or sun occurred every 19 years during the second millennium BCE when the winter moon would appear over the Heel Stone, or every 18.61 years to be precise. To calculate this interval between eclipses the priests of Stonehenge would move a stone from one hole to the next each year; 56 holes being the sum of two lots of 19 years and one of 18, which corresponds to the number of holes in the outer ditch.

From what has subsequently been learnt from prehistoric artefacts and surviving descriptions of pagan rituals it is known that the moon had great significance for the people of pre-Christian Europe, who saw it as the representation of a goddess. But it now appears that the moon may also have been a source of etheric energy which would have been focused at such sites during certain times of the year and stored in the stones for magical purposes. The high crystal content in some of the stones has given rise to speculation that they may have served a similar purpose to the pagodas of ancient China, namely as conductors for celestial and terrestrial energy, with the site itself acting as a form of amplifier.

This controversial theory has recently been given credence by two eminent physicists from London University, Professor John Taylor and Dr. Eduardo Balinovski. They measured the magnetic field of a megalith situated near Crickhowell in South Wales which revealed an intense concentration of magnetic energy. But more incredible was their discovery that they got different readings for various parts of the same stone which changes its polarity according to the configuration of the constellations.

TOUCHING THE FORCE

THOSE WHO CONSIDER themselves psychic or sensitive to earth energies and have stood within a sacred circle at dawn or at dusk will speak of having sensed the power in the stones which tingle to the touch. This sensation affirms that the person is acting as a conductor for the geodetic force, as the high priests may have done at the climax of their ceremonies in the hope of drawing revitalising energy from the earth to then bless the land with and ensure its fertility.

In his authoritative survey of pagan cults and primitive religions entitled *The White Goddess*, the English poet and novelist Robert Graves referred to a Druidic calendar which he believed had been central to the Neolithic societies (4,000–2,400 BCE) of Europe, and which hinted that the cult of the moon goddess might have been the core religion of the West. It was Graves's conclusion that the moon goddess had been worshipped as the muse of art and intuition, but was ultimately superseded by reverence for the sun god, who personified worldly knowledge and the intellect. He suggested that the increasing significance of sun worship had led Western civilisation ultimately to embrace patriarchal monotheism (the belief in one god) and with it an increasing emphasis was placed on orthodox religion in opposition to natural magic. In time, science had taken precedence over the supernatural at the cost perhaps of the psychic side of human nature.

HAVING SIFTED THROUGH some of the physical evidence and weighed the arguments it appears to me that there is no conclusive proof that the earth was visited by extraterrestrials in ancient times, but plenty to strengthen the suspicion that advocates of the ancient astronaut theory exercise their imagination more than their intellect in order to substantiate their spurious speculations. Dismissing the ancient astronaut scenario does not, of course, rule out the existence of extraterrestrial life-forms (as will be seen in Part Two), but it is unreasonable and illogical to assume that simply because we cannot account for every wonder of the ancient world that we must attribute its construction to spacemen. If extraterrestrials had visited the earth they probably couldn't have survived in our atmosphere and if our ancestors hadn't run screaming to the hills at the very sight of them they certainly wouldn't have been able to converse with them, nor convey the concept behind the monuments that they are credited with constructing.

However, the growing body of evidence to bear out the belief that our ancestors possessed a considerable degree of knowledge of astronomy, navigation and engineering might account for their marvellous monuments and it is possible that they may have inherited their skills from a far earlier civilisation. But again, we appear rather too eager to assume that this knowledge meant they possessed advanced technology, or that they had a greater understanding of the world and its workings than we do. To the contrary, the physical evidence reveals that their insights were muddled with superstition and the need to take their myths literally. They imagined themselves to be at the mercy of capricious gods who had to be appeased, whereas we have largely demystified the universe and accepted the idea that we are each responsible for our fate, and collectively responsible for the world that we inhabit. In that sense, at least, we have made some progress.

PART TWO

EXTRATERRESTRIAL ENIGMAS

Whenever the question is raised of whether or not there are extraterrestrial life-forms elsewhere in the universe, common sense, scientific fact and logic rarely bear out the argument and the discussion comes down to a question of personal belief. In Part Two I suggest that it is our perception of reality that needs to be explored rather than the frontiers of space, for the answers we seek might not be obtained by the discovery of physical evidence alone. Perhaps the truth has proven elusive because we are not dealing with a purely physical phenomenon as we had once believed.

My own UFO sightings were enough to convince me that I had seen something "alien" to my experience.

The first occurred in 1978. I was at a party in north London. It was a warm summer afternoon and

the sky was cloudless. I went out into the garden
and on looking up I saw a white light in the sky in
the middle distance. It was no ordinary light. It had
a distinct elliptical shape and after remaining
stationary for some minutes it darted around the sky
at speed in an erratic criss-cross trajectory. After
about ten minutes it shot into the sky and faded
from view. Several other witnesses to this
phenomenon agreed that its luminosity, shape and
manoeuvrability ruled out any known man-made
device or natural phenomenon such as ball lightning.

The second sighting occurred a few months later
as I walked with my father near his home on the Kent
coast one evening. The sky was cloudless and
crowded with stars. Looking up we saw three
coloured lights moving in what appeared to be close
formation. I would have dismissed them as being aircraft had they not exhibited the same erratic flight
pattern as the mysterious object that I had seen in
north London. They were travelling at too high an
altitude for us to distinguish their shapes but the
coloured light that they each emitted remained con-
stant unlike a plane which has a distinct flashing tail
or wing light.

Both of these incidents occurred after my interest
in UFOs had been aroused by Steven Spielberg's film
Close Encounters of the Third Kind. The fact that I
had experienced two sightings within months of seeing the film and none since might suggest that
intense interest in a phenomenon produces a mild
form of hysteria, during which we are keen to convince ourselves that we have experienced something
of significance. We want to believe because at that

moment society shares a common interest and we naturally want to belong. The more dramatic our experience is, the more interesting a person we appear to have become, hence the increasing incidence of alien abductions in recent years. It is no longer enough to have seen mysterious lights in the sky. If we want attention we now need physical contact.

However, my own experience has led me to believe that public interest in a phenomenon serves only to heighten our awareness of what already exists. Having had my interest in UFOs stimulated by the film I searched the skies for months afterwards in the expectation of seeing something, and I made a conscious effort to distinguish unusual objects from other lights in the sky. My neighbourhood might be visited by UFOs on a nightly basis, but not being an avid sky-watcher I couldn't possibly say for certain. Like most people I have neither the time nor the inclination to do so unless something stimulates my interest and raises my awareness from the mundane. This, I believe, is the clue to most phenomena. We are simply too wrapped up in a world of our own making to be aware of the greater reality that surrounds us.

10

CLOSE ENCOUNTER AT ROSWELL

ON 8 JULY 1947 the front page of the *Roswell Daily Record* announced the capture of a "flying saucer" which, it was claimed, had crash landed on a nearby ranch in New Mexico. This was not another hoax or scare story of the type that had been created by Orson Welles's radio dramatisation of *War of the Worlds*, but an official report issued by the U.S. army. Consequently, the news sent the national media into overdrive and UFO fever swept across the States. Then, just as suddenly as the story had broken, it was suffocated by the same information officer who had issued the initial statement, Lieutenant Walter Haut. It had all been an embarrassing mistake, he admitted. What they thought had been wreckage from a UFO was nothing more than the remains of a weather balloon. The following day at a press conference pieces of the balloon were shown to journalists who duly reported the official line. Yet no one asked how it was possible for experienced army officers to have mistaken these fragments of aluminium foil and wooden sticks for UFO wreckage, nor thought to ask how a balloon could have produced the enormous amount of debris that was known to have been found scattered over the site.

Fifty years later, after much lobbying for the truth by ufologists and intense speculation by the media, the army was forced to retract its story and admit that it had lied about the wreckage. It was not a weather balloon, it admitted, but a top secret surveillance device designed to spy on Soviet nuclear tests. But this did not satisfy the sceptics either who cited the fact that the "captured saucer" story had been sanctioned for release by the base commander, Colonel Blanchard, who would have been informed of any top secret tests in the area. The sceptics remain convinced that the government and the military had conspired to cover up the truth of the crash to avert panic and to give themselves time to study the alien technology. What other explanation could there be, they say, to account for testimonies subsequently obtained from army personnel and civilian witnesses which contradict the official line? Or the mysterious deaths of key witnesses and the disappearance of files relating to the incident—files which had been identified in an official investigation by the U.S. General Accounting Office in 1994? Even allowing for the ufologists' mistrust of official government agencies there appears to be more to the Roswell incident than had been reported at the time, much more if recent research is to be believed.

THE "COVER-UP"

THE "REAL" STORY of the crash and the subsequent cover-up began in 1978 when nuclear physicist and UFO researcher Stanton Friedman was put in touch with ex-army major Jesse Marcel. Major Marcel had been responsible for collecting the Roswell wreckage and delivering it to Wright Field army base in Ohio where captured enemy equipment was stored. He had been photographed with fragments of the balloon at the press conference the following day, but according to Friedman, he did so against his will under orders from his superiors. Roswell was then the base for America's atomic bomb unit and Marcel was its intelligence officer. He knew that the wreckage he had handled was not from a balloon. In fact, it was not like anything he had ever seen before.

Marcel had needed two vehicles to recover the vast amount of material, which was considerably more than a balloon would have produced. It had been scattered over a 1-kilometre area in a manner which Marcel later described as being characteristic of an object that had exploded above the ground while travelling at a high speed. "It was quite obvious to me," he explained, "familiar with air activities, that it was not a weather balloon, nor was it a plane or a missile."

On the way back to the base Major Marcel stopped off at his home to show the debris to his wife and young son Jesse, which he was unlikely to have done had the debris been from a balloon or a secret military probe. The boy remembered seeing his father in a highly excitable state, which seems unlikely had the wreckage been of terrestrial origin. Jesse has spoken of seeing fragments of metal foil with a less reflective surface than aluminium which a colleague of his father had tried in vain to dent with a sledge-hammer. He also described handling lightweight beams between 30 and 45 centimetres in length which were embossed with geometric symbols.

The following morning the crash site was cordoned off and cleared of the remaining fragments while Lieutenant Haut drafted the press release announcing the recovery of a crashed UFO. According to Stanton Friedman it was Haut's rash action which prompted a knee-jerk reaction from Acting Director of Strategic Air Command General McMullen in Washington. When news of the incident reached McMullen he ordered Colonel Dubose, Chief of Staff at Fort Worth, to concoct a cover story which Fried-man claims "launched the U.S. government on a long-term campaign of disinformation." In defence of his action Dubose is quoted as saying: "We had just gone through a world war . . . then came this flying saucer business. It was just too much for the public to have to deal with."

After the army had quashed all rumours of a flying saucer crash with the weather balloon story, Major Marcel was allegedly ordered not to speak to anyone and in turn pressured his wife and son to promise to keep secret what they had seen. Not even their closest friends were to be told and especially not any strangers.

Lieutenant Haut was also ordered not to comment on the cover story, although he too was convinced that the UFO wreckage was genuine. He recently remarked that there was "no chance that the wreckage could have come from a balloon" adding, "A balloon may have crashed but it certainly had nothing to do with the downed saucer."

ALIEN BODIES

IF INDEED THERE had been a UFO crash at Roswell it raises the obvious question: "Were there aliens aboard and, if so, what happened to the bodies?" Friedman believes he found the answer when he interviewed Glenn Dennis, a mortician employed by the Ballard Funeral Home which served as a mortuary for the base.

Dennis claims that in July 1947 he had been consulted by the army who asked how they could deal with "small bodies." These could, of course, have been monkeys which had been used as test pilots or had been killed during a secret experiment, but it is highly unlikely that the army would have consulted a mortician about bodies which they could easily dispose of themselves. Dennis claims to have been forcibly evicted from the base on his next visit when he went to see if he could help with the bodies. He also claims to have made contact with a nurse at the base who had caught a glimpse of an autopsy being carried out on two small, hairless corpses with slits where their ears, nose and mouth would be. They had brown-grey skin, four fingers but no thumb. When Dennis attempted to contact the nurse again he was told that she had emigrated to England, but after obtaining her new address he says that his letters were returned, marked "deceased."

Interest in the Roswell incident intensified after the broadcast of a TV documentary in NBC's Unsolved Mysteries series in 1989, which attracted 28 million viewers in the U.S., and the subsequent publication of a slew of books on the subject. These included Friedman's impeccably researched *Crash at Corona* (co-authored with aviation expert Don Berliner), which collated interviews with 92 military personnel and civilians who claimed to have been concerned with the crash.

One of these witnesses was an anonymous ex-army/air force photographer (who insisted on being identified only by his initials, F.B.). He stated that he had been flown from his base at the Anacostia Naval Air Station in Washington, D.C., to Roswell a couple of days after the supposed crash where he was told to photograph the remains of four alien bodies that had been found near the wreckage. The photographs have never been published, but the photographer's description of the bodies is strikingly similar to the description given by mortician Glenn Dennis, and to the bodies seen in what is thought to be official footage of an alien autopsy unearthed in 1992 and subsequently televised to a worldwide audience of millions in 1995. A number of military personnel who were involved with the Roswell incident are said to have identified the alien in the autopsy footage as being the same creature that they saw, but the owner of the film, record producer Ray Santilli, claims that the cameraman told him that he took the shots on 31 May 1947 near Socorro, New Mexico. The implication being that there were two fatal incidents in the region.

THE ALIEN "AUTOPSY"

IN THE CLIMATE of intense interest that followed the discovery of the autopsy footage in 1993 several key questions went unanswered and many anomalies were never satisfactorily explained. The film had been unearthed in Ohio in 1993 by Ray Santilli during a search for previously unreleased footage of Elvis Presley. Santilli claims to have bought the Presley footage from an ex-forces cameraman called Jack Barnett who then offered him the autopsy footage. But investigations by a French TV journalist revealed that the real source of the Presley footage had been Ohio radio DJ Bill Randle who admitted that he had hired Barnett to make the autopsy film, which implies that it was a fake. Barnett died in 1967 and therefore could not have sold the footage to Santilli in 1993. When Santilli was confronted with these facts he altered his statement, claiming that "Barnett" was an assumed name for the real photographer who was evidently camera-shy.

The age of the film itself has also been called into question after Santilli claimed that Kodak had verified that the roll had been manufactured in 1947. Kodak subsequently denied having received any samples for testing and revealed that identity markings which Santilli said were to be seen on the edge of the film could also have been found on film manufactured in 1927 and 1967.

An independent investigation by the German UFO researcher Michael Hesemann revealed that two three-frame sequences had been submitted to photographic expert Bob Shell, an ex-FBI consultant, for analysis and that he was unable to pin down the exact year of manufacture, but was convinced that it was some time before 1958. The only problem was that the samples did not show any aliens and could therefore have come from a different roll of film.

Further investigations punched more holes in the anonymous photographer's story as a succession of retired combat cameramen lent their expertise to the debate. They all agreed that there would have been no reason to fly a photographer from Washington as there would have been several stationed in New Mexico, including one at the Roswell army air field. Furthermore, they pointed out that after the war, army autopsies were shot in colour as a matter of routine, whereas the alien autopsy was filmed in black and white in a shaky, amateurish fashion that no military cameraman would have been allowed to do. Dismissing the film as a fake, ex-combat cameraman Joe Longo has said: "If anybody in my unit shot film in that manner, he'd be back scrubbing pots in the kitchen."

As for the footage itself there are a number of significant irregularities in the autopsy procedure and inconsistencies regarding the appearance of the bodies which suggest that the film is a hoax. Special-effects experts have pointed to the fact that anatomical details are consistent with a dummy cast from a person who was standing at the time the mould was made and do not conform to those of a corpse. An American pathologist, Dr. Ed Uthman, had harsh words too for the doctors' performances which he likened to actors who were clearly uncomfortable in front of the camera. Dr. Uthman pointed out that their incisions were far too tentative for professional pathologists who would have been more methodical, cutting "deeper and faster."

Crucial sequences showing the skin flaps being folded back are missing which special-effects experts suggest is because the body was probably made from latex rubber which wrinkles on being manipulated in that fashion. There is also a missing sequence between the sawing of the skull and the removal of the "alien" brain which, again, indicates that a pause was needed, in this case to pop the brain into the empty skull.

But most damning of all perhaps is a small but significant detail of the kind that would lead to the unmasking of the guilty party in a fictional murder mystery. One of the last shots shows a close-up of the film canister with the date "July 1947" and the legend "Process Internally" clearly marked. What someone appears to have overlooked is the fact that the official Department of Defense seal did not come into use until many years later!

11

WERE THE MOON
LANDINGS FAKED?

WHEN AMERICAN ASTRONAUT Neil Armstrong
became the first man to walk on the moon on 20 July 1969,
an estimated 600 million people around the world witnessed the historic event on television. For many it was a
dream come true, the moment when mankind finally freed
itself from being earthbound and was poised to explore the
frontiers of space. There was a shared sense of pride in a
great achievement which found expression in Armstrong's
immortal words: "That's one small step for man, one giant
leap for mankind."

However, in the euphoria of the moment few noticed a
number of anomalies in NASA's official photographs
which have yet to be satisfactorily explained. Nor did anyone think to question how certain crucial obstacles to a
manned moon landing had been miraculously and mysteri-

ously overcome just in time for the deadline imposed by President Kennedy.

NASA is known to have carried out a feasibility study in the early 60s which is said to have revealed a less than 1 per cent chance of success. Yet by the end of the decade, we are led to believe that men landed on the moon in a rocket whose computer had less processing power than a modern pocket calculator. It was only after the Apollo programme was phased out, following the final mission to the moon in December 1972, that the evidence was closely analysed by those who suspected that the moon landings might have been faked.

THE X-RAY FACTOR

IN ORDER TO reach the moon the astronauts had to pass beyond the Van Allen Belt, a protective barrier of charged particles created by cosmic rays which have been trapped by the earth's magnetic fields. This natural phenomenon shields the earth from the sun's lethal radiation. Once beyond this barrier the crew would be exposed to intense and sustained doses of radiation with only a thin lead lining in the rocket to shield them. NASA has never explained how they overcame this fundamental problem.

Prior to Apollo 11 all of America's manned missions had orbited just a few hundred miles above the earth, safely within this ceiling. Some of the conspiracy theorists have seized on this fact and suggest that Apollo 11 did not go beyond the Van Allen Belt, but simply circled the earth until the scheduled splashdown. They suspect that the moon landing was faked by NASA which was under intense pressure to put a man on the moon by the end of the 60s to meet President Kennedy's much publicised deadline. For propaganda purposes America had to be seen to have beaten the Russians in the space race while NASA knew that its future funding depended on success. Whether or not NASA scientists overcame this fundamental problem in time for later landings is still a matter of intense debate and speculation among sceptics.

THE PHOTOGRAPHIC EVIDENCE

MORE CONCRETE EVIDENCE of a cover-up is said to be found in the official NASA photographs of the Apollo 11 landing and also of later missions which, if true, suggests a continuing conspiracy to deceive the public.

If anyone was foolish enough to store photographic film in their freezer and then grill it in the oven after taking their pictures they would not expect to see very good results. But that is effectively how the astronauts treated their film when they took it from an area of deep shade into the brilliant sunlight on the surface of the moon where temperatures vary from one extreme to the other. It is not unreasonable to assume that the extreme temperatures would have made it impossible to load the film which would have been fused into a sticky morass. Moreover, photographic film is highly sensitive to X-rays, as anyone unfortunate enough to have had their holiday snaps "fogged" by the early airport security systems will know to their cost. The astronauts' shots should have been adversely affected by the sun's radiation in a similar way during the journey beyond the Belt, but they were all perfect. Perhaps too perfect. On the Apollo 11 mission Armstrong and his colleague Buzz Aldrin were fitted with professional, fixed-focus Hasselblad cameras strapped to their chests which had 250mm telephoto lenses and viewfinders on the top. The procedure for loading a Hasselblad with film is similar to that which was used in the earliest days of photography when changing old-fashioned photographic plates. It is a delicate and tricky operation which requires steady hands and nimble fingers. The Apollo astronauts wore thick rubber gloves which would have made reloading quite a problem.

But perhaps the most puzzling aspect are the shadows cast by the astronauts and their equipment which do not appear to conform to the conditions under which the photographs were said to have been taken. NASA claims that the only light source was the sun and yet in the famous shot showing Armstrong and Aldrin planting the US flag on the moon's surface they cast unequal shadows whilst standing only a few feet apart. Another shot, showing Aldrin on his own with Armstrong and the lunar module reflected in his visor, is suspect for a number of reasons. The first is that the shadow on Aldrin's right side is too light for the greater contrast that is characteristic of the moon. The sun on his left should put his right side into deep shade and yet we can clearly see every wrinkle on his spacesuit. More curiously, the terrain behind Aldrin fades into darkness but it should be quite distinct all the way to the horizon as there is no atmosphere on the moon to affect the light. NASA has explained this phenomenon by pointing out that photographic film can make distant objects seem darker the further they are away from the camera. However, this argument has not convinced the sceptics who claim to have identified a whole catalogue of curious details including a mysterious object reflected in Aldrin's visor in the same photograph. It can be seen clearly against the blackness above the horizon where one might expect to glimpse a piece of film equipment if the shots had been faked in the studio.

If the shots had been faked in a studio this would also explain why details such as the United States nameplates on the side of the lunar module are highlighted when they should be in deep shade as there is no refracted light on the moon and the sun was streaming in from the opposite side. The same anomaly can be seen in shots from subsequent missions which photographic experts say suggests the presence of more than one light source as would be present in a film studio.

Other oddities include the absence of stars in the sky in many of the official space agency photographs. According to Maria Blyzinsky, Curator of Astronomy at the Greenwich Observatory in London, the lack of atmosphere on the moon should make these clearly visible, although NASA counters this argument by claiming that the sunlight was so strong that it obscured the light from the stars. Photographs from later missions reveal other peculiarities such as the lack of scorch marks and a crater under the lunar module which one would expect to have been created by the rocket on landing.

These unexplained irregularities make a convincing case for the photos having been faked, but there is one piece of concrete evidence for which the conspiracy theorists do not have a ready explanation—the 340kg piece of radioactive moon rock which NASA proudly displayed for the scrutiny of the public and independent experts on the astronauts' return. Geologists found less silica and aluminium than would be found in rocks from earth and considerably more magnesium, iron and titanium which left them in no doubt that these samples came from an extraterrestrial source.

COCK-UP OR COVER-UP?

ONE THEORY WHICH no one seems to have considered is the possibility that the landings did take place, but that NASA was embarrassed when its film did not survive the journey for the reasons already stated. In its desperation to satisfy public expectation, exploit its propaganda coup and secure its future funding it foolishly faked photographs in a studio, perhaps where the landing had previously been rehearsed. Or maybe photographs taken during those rehearsals were used.

A similar scenario was featured in the 1978 movie *Capricorn One*, and in the 1971 James Bond film *Diamonds Are Forever*. This suggests that the rumour of the faked photos had been circulating among film technicians and found its way into fiction, or that an informer was leaking the information in a form which might get the public guessing. If so, they certainly succeeded.

12
LIFE OUT THERE

BELIEF IN THE existence of extraterrestrials comes, like most things, in degrees. Most believers have been convinced by the impressive amount of anecdotal evidence and out-of-focus films and photos. Few, if any, could have their convictions shaken by sceptics, although they have probably never had a close encounter themselves. In extreme cases an individual can express their belief with the frightening intensity, blind faith and attendant paranoia of a religious fanatic. For these reasons it is difficult to find an objective believer and rarer still to find one who understands the scientific basis for the existence of aliens and the practicalities of interstellar travel. Science writer Michael White, author of *The Science of the X Files* and *Life Out There*, is that rare exception. He makes a convincing argument against the possibility of interstellar travel and the existence of alien visitors to earth.

"I don't rule it out entirely, but it is impractical in two respects. One is that interstellar travel is a very difficult thing to accomplish, which is not to say it hasn't been done because there may be extraterrestrial civilisations tens of thousands of years in advance of our own and I would hope that humans will be able to travel such distances in five or ten thousand years. But a stronger argument is that we simply aren't important enough to warrant such attention from extraterrestrials. As far as we know we are a fairly insignificant planet—unless there is something special about our planet of which we aren't aware at this moment. We are just one of a billion planets in our galaxy and I just don't see why we should be visited all the time!

"There are countless millions of galaxies out there so the odds in favour of the universe teeming with intelligent life is high. Some of them must have the technology to travel to other worlds, but I don't accept the idea that they are coming to earth on a regular basis and in such vast numbers as the reported sightings would suggest. Astronomers have yet to identify any habitable planets close enough to our galaxy to make travel a practical proposition.

"I can believe that they came once or twice in ancient times and that these visits were recorded in the mythology of early civilisations and in some of the visions detailed in the Bible, but it's arrogant of us and illogical to suppose that they are swarming around our airspace because we are so incredibly interesting or significant. Nor do I believe in all the alleged abduction cases because they are totally illogical. They are just an ego trip for the alleged abductees."

That's fine from an intellectual point of view, but what if the laws of science, which are constantly being amended as man's understanding and knowledge grows, don't apply elsewhere in the cosmos?

"Science has proven that its laws do operate throughout the cosmos. We call it homogeneity. It is actually the first law of science and says that what happens here, happens 'out there' too. That's because we have all evolved from the same Big Bang. The material that is in a star a billion light years away is roughly the same mixture of material of which we and the earth are made. The same 111 basic elements are everywhere. There is no mystery 'element X' that will undo or contradict the laws we have established as operating throughout the universe. Astronomers know about the mixture of matter on other distant stars for a fact, without having to go there, by means of spectroscopy which involves analysing their spectrum of radiation. From studying the movements of stars we are also able to say that the same forces that are at work there are also at work in our solar system. So there are no strange laws which can be broken by an advanced race. The same laws which make interstellar travel impossible for us at the moment will apply equally to them.

"The only way they could travel vast distances at the necessary speed to make a mission viable would be if they could find a loophole in those laws. And there are only two ways they might be able to do that. One is by using wormholes [tunnels in the geometry of space–time which are assumed to exist connecting different regions of the universe] and the other is by hyperspace travel, or surfing, which basically involves the craft contracting the space in front of it and expanding the space behind it, as in *Star Trek* when the USS *Enterprise* goes into warp drive. There is nothing actually wrong with either idea, they are both possibilities within the laws of general relativity, but the craft would have to distort the space–time continuum like a tiny black hole. Even scientists don't understand how it would work in practice. The major problem with hyperspace travel is that it would require a phenomenal amount of power to work—the equivalent energy to that produced by the sun during its entire lifetime! Of course, there may be other ways that we don't know about yet, just as we didn't know about those two methods ourselves a few years ago. So I'm not ruling anything out."

What if matter vibrates at a different frequency in other, less dense dimensions allowing more evolved beings and the crafts they have created to circumvent the limitations of our physical world?

"I have to say that for a scientist there are only four dimensions, although there is a mathematical concept which allows for 26 more, but this is theoretical and doesn't actually mean that we accept the existence of parallel universes or anything like that. When people use expressions such as 'other dimensions' it's always a vague, mystical idea. When you press them to say what they really mean by it they never can. Science doesn't accept the idea that matter vibrates at different frequencies. The argument that a higher form of life might exist outside of our dimension following the same principles that allow matter to change form in our physical world doesn't stand up to scrutiny.

"Here on earth, ice can be transformed to water and then to steam, but that doesn't prove that matter has been altered by the frequency of its vibration. What has happened is that a change has been made to the bonds between the H_2O molecules. Ice is a very compact form with a crystalline structure while water has fewer of these bonds, and in steam there are even less so the H_2O floats around on its own as vapour. That has nothing to do with vibration. The only vibration that scientists really think about is with regard to temperature. If you heat a metal rod, for example, the atoms vibrate faster and carry the energy along the rod so that if you are holding it you will get burnt. But that's conduction."

Can Michael imagine a time in the not too distant future when science and the paranormal are reconciled?

"No, because they seem to be drifting further and further apart all the time. When you look at the different aspects of quantum mechanics, which is on the fringes of science, the language seems to be almost mystical, and yet if you talk to those scientists they dismiss UFOs and paranormal phenomena out of hand. The reasons for this are firstly, they believe there is definitely an elitism at the 'cutting edge' of science, but only derision to be had for taking the paranormal seriously. Secondly, they cannot accept anything that is not presentable in mathematical terms. And lastly, they hate the thought of people who have not gone through the agonies of learning science explaining the existence of UFOs and the paranormal in pseudo-scientific terms which are invariably inaccurate."

Perhaps they are also uncomfortable with the possibility that people with no scientific training might have acquired superior knowledge through contact with more highly evolved beings? "I'm not comfortable with the concept of channelling."

Maybe not, but Michael's fascinating and eminently readable "alternative" biography of Isaac Newton, *The Last Sorcerer*, suggests that only by reconciling science and the supernatural can we make the enormous leap of consciousness men like Einstein and Newton made to bring our modern world into being. Michael's arguments are very convincing, and he himself has revealed that Newton frequently used alchemy and magic in his studies. He also notes that a third of the 1,700 books in Newton's library were concerned with magic and alchemy, and that the great man actually renounced all scientific endeavour at the age of 53. To which we could add Michael's own personal experience of the paranormal which he still can't explain.

It occurred during a long, hot summer holiday in 1974 when he was 15 years old. A group of his school friends had been messing about with a ouija board and claimed to have succeeded in contacting an entity which identified itself as an alien living on Saturn. Michael, ever sceptical but curious, was roped in, apparently at the alien's request, for a special "solo" session with just one other member of the group—a friend he trusted implicitly not to play tricks on him. Within a few minutes the glass began to glide effortlessly across the table while both boys' fingers hovered just above it. After answering a few general questions about the group, the "alien contact" ended the session leaving each boy stunned and exhilarated. Yet still neither could accept the possibility that what they had witnessed could have been a genuine phenomenon.

After leaving school Michael and his friend didn't see each other for 20 years, but recently they bumped into each other again. "And he still maintains that he did not move the glass across the Ouija board," Michael says, somewhat bemused.

> "I don't believe that we were contacted by aliens or mischievous spirits, nor can I accept that we were practising psychokinesis. But I want to understand this and other phenomena. That's why I continue to be curious and keep an open mind. I still can't account for it. All I can suggest is that human beings might have some latent ability to affect matter with their own minds. But that poses another problem. The energy, or current, needed to move a light object such as an empty glass a metre across a table is more than the circuit board of the human brain can handle. It would literally fry our brains!"

That may be, but psychics, healers and mystically inclined ufologists would argue that those who work with the paranormal are merely channelling energy far greater than their own. And that it does not originate with them or manifest in the physical world at all.

> "I could accept that possibility. I don't dismiss everything to do with UFOs and the paranormal. I'd like these things to be true. It would make life more exciting. I'm perfectly prepared to say that these things could happen, but that we don't know enough at this stage to explain how they happen. So, I'm keeping an open mind."

13

ALIEN ABDUCTIONS

ON THE EVENING of 27 October 1974 John and Sue Day and their three children were driving back to their home in Avely, Essex after visiting Sue's parents when their ten-year-old son saw a blue, oval-shaped light in the sky. Within moments the car was shrouded in a green mist and everything became eerily quiet. Then the car radio began to spark and smoulder. John frantically tugged at the wires to prevent a fire and a moment later the engine cut out. After what seemed like a few seconds there was a jolt and the car kicked into life again. The road ahead was clear and the light in the sky had gone, but for a moment in the darkness John sensed that Sue was no longer beside him. "Is everybody here?" he asked. But as soon as the words had left his lips he noticed that she was sitting there as before.

The family might have forgotten all about the incident had they not discovered that they had "lost" two hours which they could not account for. The journey from Sue's parents should have taken them no more than 40 minutes and yet, instead of arriving home just before 11pm, they arrived home at 1am, having left about 10:15. They did not suspect any kind of extraterrestrial connection as there were no known incidents of alien abduction in Britain at that time and the relatively few cases on record in America were not public knowledge. It was only after the success of the film *Close Encounters of the Third Kind* in 1979 that UFOs became implanted in the public consciousness.

The Days tried to put the incident out of their minds, but over the following weeks the family began to exhibit subtle but significant transformations in their personalities. John and Sue became more self-confident and John began to write poetry as if something had just removed a block to his creativity. The couple became more conscious of their health and changed overnight to a strict vegetarian diet. They went off alcohol and John gave up smoking, an addiction he had repeatedly struggled to overcome in the past but which he was now able to throw off with ease. Their ten-year-old son, who had been categorised at school as being a slow reader, made an inexplicable improvement and their youngest child declared an ambition to build a spacecraft that would take thousands of people away from the violence and pollution on earth. Whatever it was that had occurred in those missing two hours was no longer important to them for they all seemed to have benefited in some way. But then more disconcerting things began to occur.

The family began to experience a catalogue of curious and unaccountable incidents in their home characteristic of poltergeist activity. There were strange smells, objects which mysteriously disappeared only to reappear just as mysteriously a few days later, and doors flew open by themselves. In desperation John contacted a UFO researcher whom he had heard being interviewed on the radio and invited him to witness the poltergeist activity. The researcher was impressed and recommended John to a hypnotherapist called Leonard Wilder who was able to draw out the memory of those missing two hours in a series of sessions.

The fact that the majority of abduction "memories" are drawn out by hypnotherapists, rather than being recalled by the alleged abductee, makes them somewhat suspect. This is not to suggest that the individual is deliberately fantasising, but rather that their memory of the experience is subjective. As UFO researcher Robert Sheaffer says in *The UFO Verdict*:

> "Psychologists generally agree that what a person says under hypnosis need not necessarily be actual fact, but rather represents what the person believes to have happened. Hypnosis is of little value in separating fact from fantasy."

John's initial recollections were apparently enough to trigger spontaneous "memories" from Sue who later agreed to undergo regression therapy with Wilder. By the end of these sessions the full story of the Days' "abduction" had emerged.

John described being enveloped in an intense white light and he recalled a floating feeling as he was taken up and out of the car. The next thing he remembered was being in a huge structure like an aircraft hangar, which appears to have been a loading bay in the alien spacecraft. He was looking down on his own car from a balcony and could see Sue and himself apparently asleep in the front and the children in the back. Sue also recalled the hangar, and standing on the balcony with John and their ten-year-old son, but when she looked down at the car she was sure she saw John and the boy standing outside the vehicle, not asleep inside. It may be significant that both the sense of floating and the experience of bilocation (being in two places simultaneously) are indicative of an out-of-body experience (see page 211).

John was then led to an examination room where he was scanned and prodded with small, blunt instruments by two ugly dwarf-like beings while three tall creatures in silver suits watched with apparent interest. Afterwards he was given a guided tour of the spacecraft during which no words were spoken but ideas were communicated to him by telepathy. In the control room he was treated to a pictorial trip through the solar system on a large movie screen and was shown a holographic image of a planet that had been decimated by pollution, which he took to be a warning of what might happen to earth if we continue on our present self-destructive course of behaviour. He was then taken to what might have been a holding cell or transporter room and from there he found himself back in the car, though he did not recall how he got there.

Sue claims to have had a similar experience. She was subjected to a thorough physical examination after which she was given a tour of the craft and shown the pictures of earth as seen from space. Curiously, after having seen her home planet she expressed a wish to stay on the ship and the aliens agreed. It was only when she saw her husband returning to the car that she changed her mind and asked to go back. This delay may explain why John feared that he had returned without her.

Another curious consequence of their close encounter was that John Day soon found far more rewarding employment which satisfied his need for self-expression, although he had to lose his previous job in the process. Recurrent nightmares and the unsettling poltergeist activity had driven him to the verge of a nervous breakdown, but from this crisis he emerged with a clearer picture of what he wanted out of life and he got it. As for the poltergeist activity, it would appear that the abduction experience stimulated the family's innate psychic energies albeit in a random and rather unsettling manner.

EXTENSIVE EXPERIENCES

SUCH EXPERIENCES ARE more common than one might imagine. There are several thousand cases of alleged alien abductions on record, all of which date from the late 1940s when American businessman Kenneth Arnold reported sighting the first "flying saucer" of modern times on 24 June 1947. But the first written account of an encounter with strange beings from the sky goes back to the 19th century when Archbishop Agobard of Lyons recorded the case of four people whom a mob wanted to stone to death for claiming that they had met strangers from a country in the clouds. The Archbishop successfully argued that such a belief was contrary to common sense and the penitent "witnesses" recanted before the crowd who in turn were persuaded to spare their lives.

The second half of the 20th century saw UFO sightings outnumber stories of hauntings and other more traditional psychic phenomena, leading to the theory that extraterrestrials might be unconscious projections of the human mind which needs to find expression for other states of consciousness in a socially acceptable context.

By 1991 the intensity of public interest in the phenomenon prompted the first serious scientific survey. Budd
Hopkins and David Jacobs of the Roper organisation asked
a random sample of nearly 6,000 American adults if they
recalled seeing strange lights in their bedroom at any time,
if they had missed brief periods of their lives that they
could not account for, or had woken in the night to find
mysterious figures moving around their bed. The pollsters
found that 119, or 2 per cent, could recall one or more incidents of this nature which, if taken as being typical of the
population, would equate to 5 million Americans. Even if
it is spurious to extrapolate the figures in this fashion it still
leaves a huge number of people who are convinced that
they have had some form of close encounter with extraterrestrials. Either the human race is being systematically
hijacked wholesale by aliens on a nightly basis by a vast
armada of spaceships, or our preoccupation with the mysteries of the universe has somehow produced a form of
mass hysteria in our collective consciousness.

THE ALIENS AMONG US

UFOLOGIST GREGORY VAN DYK, author of *The Alien
Files*, is convinced that such abduction stories are true and
that extraterrestrials are already among us, hidden from
view by our limited perception and our rational,
conventional minds.

> "The principal difference is that my hypothesis concerns
> the faulty way in which we view the nature of reality. I
> suggest that the extraterrestrial visitors operate on a
> higher level of vibration to us and so are generally invis-

ible, although the sightings and contacts are real. I suspect that the majority of contacts are actually made on this mental or psychic level, yet it leaves such an impression on the contactees or abductees that they are convinced it could only have been physical. A good example of this is the case of an Australian woman who claimed to have been abducted at the very moment she was seen by two witnesses to be standing in a field talking to herself. They observed her appearing to interact with an object and its occupants while in some sort of trance, and yet the two witnesses saw nothing 'other worldly' at all."

Van Dyk also quotes from the conclusions of Dr. Kenneth Ring, Professor of Psychology at the University of Connecticut, who suggests that abductions are essentially out-of-body experiences which take place in a finer dimension. Van Dyk appears to share Ring's conclusion that we enter this dimension naturally every night during sleep when our spirit, or ethereal, body separates from its physical shell to receive instruction from higher beings, some of whom could be extraterrestrials.

"I'm questioning the mistake we make in trying to apply physical principles and scientific laws to something which experience suggests is largely spirit-based. Extraterrestrials could be made of finer matter and exist in a different dimension where their molecules vibrate at a different frequency just as sound and light do. Unfortunately, scientists are like trainspotters: their whole view of reality is matter-based which is a false criterium. If we adopt a spirit-based view so many of these sightings and abductions can be easily and satisfactorily explained.

"I actually began my research with a completely open mind, but in the end I was overwhelmed by the evidence and convinced of the reality of extraterrestrial life and alien abductions."

So, what would Van Dyk say to the cynics who love to point out that astronomers spend years peering through telescopes without a glimpse of a UFO, while many UFO enthusiasts claim to see them on a regular basis?

"Who says the astronomers don't see them? Perhaps they do and they don't recognise them for what they are because they don't want to believe such things exist. It wouldn't do their credibility or chance of funding any favours, would it? Most of them have tunnel vision. Or perhaps officials got to them first.

"Of the purely physical contacts, it appears that the only reason we don't have tangible proof is that governments have been putting pressure on the witnesses to keep silent and have confiscated the fragments that have been found. And yet, despite their best efforts these stories still come out—eventually.

"I think it's possible that the alien craft only come within our perception range when they alter frequency on entering our airspace at which point certain UFO enthusiasts might be more sensitive to seeing them without being aware that they are practising a form of psychic sight. That would explain why some people see them while they remain invisible to others."

But once we start putting UFOs into the metaphysical bag

isn't there the danger that ufology will become as irrational as some religious cults which are based on blind faith?

"It's not as black and white as that. In the course of my research I met and spoke with the American transceiver, or medium, Lyssa Royale who claims to have contact with three extraterrestrials in physical form and another one which describes itself as a group consciousness. I was struck by her sincerity and the quality of the information she was receiving."

Had Van Dyk considered the possibility that being psychic, these channellers may instead be simply indulging the fantasies of their own subconscious or perhaps even linking in to discarnate beings on the astral plane who enjoy deceiving them?

"Yes, I was aware that some of what Lyssa was channelling was coloured by her own culture and her subconscious, but the essence of what she was receiving seemed valid. In my opinion there isn't a fundamental difference between extraterrestrial entities and discarnate beings on the astral or lower levels of existence, and the channellers themselves don't seem to be able to tell the difference between the two. They can't be sure about the source so you have to judge who they are by what they say. The beings that come through these transceivers are often very specific about who they are, where they are from and what their purpose is in making contact, so it seems genuine. You have to accept channelling as a source equally valid as the abduction witnesses. Channellers may be the group who ultimately solve this whole enigma."

Van Dyk believes that the alien species known commonly as the Greys have embarked on a wholesale abduction project on earth because they are suffering from a genetic defect which threatens the existence of the species. He says that we only have to look at their stunted growth and discoloured skin for proof of this. Van Dyk also implies that their actions prove they are less evolved, or spiritually advanced, than we are and yet, if that is the case how could they have developed the necessary technology required for interstellar travel?

> "I'm uncomfortable with the expression 'spiritually advanced' because in our culture it is equated with mumbo-jumbo. I prefer to think that, regardless of their spiritual advancement, the Greys have a capability that we have not yet discovered. The matter of which they are made simply vibrates at a different frequency to ours— in other respects, however, they do appear to be a lower order of beings to humans.
>
> "They seem to believe that we are untainted by this defect because we have not been interacting with extraterrestrials and as such are prime breeding stock. But logically it's an experiment doomed to failure as it is the equivalent of trying to cross-breed mules with thoroughbreds."

If the Greys are abducting humans on the scale Van Dyk is suggesting, how is it that the abductees are never able to describe the technology involved in the examinations or experiments? Even allowing for the fact that a sterile operating theatre would probably be as sparse as that in a human hospital is it not unreasonable to expect an abductee to remember a few telling details?

"I don't agree. If you are wheeled into an operating theatre and sedated you won't remember more than a bright
light over your head and afterwards you'd be too groggy
and unfocused to take in much detail. Nevertheless a few
people have described their surroundings in some detail.
Abductee Betty Andreasson was able to describe the
alien propulsion unit with its three rotating glass balls
and the vacuum they generated, so it's wrong to say there
are no details. But they are very rare."

The case of Betty Andreasson, who claimed to have been
abducted from her home in Massachusetts in January
1967, is a significant one. Like many others it has clear
parallels with what an embryo experiences in the womb
and as such it is often cited as an example of an abduction
fantasy triggered by unconscious memories of the time
before birth. Betty recalled sitting in a transparent chair
which was filled with a grey fluid and being fed sweet
liquid through a tube in her mouth. She also claimed to
have floated through a series of womb-like rooms and
along tunnels which sound suspiciously like representations of the birth canal.

  If she had really been a captive in a flying saucer would
her captors have allowed her to drift freely and unaccom-
panied through their craft?

ALTERED STATES

AUTHOR AND UFO investigator Jenny Randles has a wider
perspective on the abduction phenomenon.

"I don't believe that there are hordes of extraterrestrials
engaged in physically abducting human beings. From
my research and the many personal interviews that I have
conducted with people who claim to have had experiences of this nature I have concluded that the alleged
abductions appear to involve a communication with
another intelligence during an altered state of consciousness. I have identified several different possible explanations for these experiences none of which involve the
physical transportation of human beings aboard spacecraft. That I am certain of."

According to Randles, all UFO sightings and abductions
fall into four main categories: external events with mundane causes, external events with exotic causes, internal
events with mundane causes and internal events with
exotic causes.

In the first category we have sightings of natural phenomena such as Venus, the brightest star in the night sky,
which is frequently misinterpreted as a UFO by people
who don't recognise it, or who are unaware of the visual
tricks it can play under certain atmospheric conditions.

In the second category we have what are known as
Unidentified Atmospheric Phenomena (UAPs) which may
account for the curious fact that so many alleged sightings
take place around fault lines. UAPs could also account for
all manner of tingling sensations, heaviness in the
atmosphere and electrical phenomena which the witnesses
have described. But it is also possible that an as yet
unknown form of atmospheric energy triggers a form of
alien contact which some people perceive as being a
physical reality. And then there are the more science
fiction-type scenarios which should also be considered, if

only for the sake of completeness. These include the remote possibility that the "visitors" could be time travellers from our own future or that they are the product of secret government agency mind control experiments. It is a fact that U.S. defence agencies have experimented with "behaviour modification" for more than 30 years and it has been suggested that the psychotropic weapons (drugs which act on the mind) used in such tests in the USA and Britain could have induced images of spaceships and aliens as a side-effect. And then, of course, we have the distinct possibility that a proportion of contacts with extraterrestrial intelligences is genuine, if only because it is a statistical certainty that some of the trillions of stars in our ever-expanding universe can sustain some form of life. However, the vast distances involved make it more likely that contact is telepathic rather than physical for reasons stated elsewhere in this book.

The third category, internal events with mundane causes, covers hoaxing, false memory syndrome, various altered states of consciousness, sleep paralysis, "false awakening" dreams, lucid dreams and hallucinations (which more than three-quarters of the population will have experienced at least once in their lifetime, according to Dr. Ronald Siegel of the UCLA School of Medicine).

The fourth category, internal events with exotic causes, includes the possibility that certain close encounters are merely projections from what Carl Jung, the Swiss psychoanalyst, called "the collective unconscious." This is a plasmic mind field inhabited by creatures of myth, human archetypes and symbolic representations of our thoughts and feelings which are a shared experience of our species.

Another possibility is that alien contacts are a subjective reality which the alleged abductee interprets in these

terms because, to a degree, it is currently socially acceptable to do so. In earlier times the witness may have
expressed the experience in religious symbolism, such as a
vision of the Virgin Mary or angelic beings, but these tend
to be seen by secular society as symptoms of a hysterical
or neurotic nature.

Evidently there are plenty of rational explanations to be
explored before a serious investigator even considers the
possibility of physical abduction by aliens.

So how does Randles account for the physical scars
which some abductees have produced as evidence of the
alleged alien experiments? Could these too be manifestations of the unconscious mind?

> "In each and every one of the 50 cases that I have person-
> ally investigated in Britain I have never come across scars
> that could have any connection with extraterrestrials. It
> is my opinion that in cases where a supposed abductee
> has found wounds on their body all they have done is dis-
> cover marks that they had not previously noticed. I'm
> sure that if you made a cross comparison with the rest of
> the population you would find many people who would
> discover cuts and bruises that they had not noticed
> before. Unless someone puts the idea into their mind
> that they might have been abducted and then asks them
> to look for physical evidence, they won't find it. Some of
> these experiences appear to take place when the individ-
> ual is in a catatonic trance-like state. It is a process sim-
> ilar to sleepwalking and in such a state they can cause
> themselves an injury which they will have no recollection
> of and have no explanation for when they wake."

It is Randles's opinion that abductees share certain personality characteristics which could be considered a form of psychic sensitivity which predisposes them to such experiences.

"There are what I call abduction-prone personalities who are anything but neurotic or overly imaginative as some cynics might assume. They are, in fact, remarkably gifted and it is this capacity for visual creativity and better than average recall which I believe is the key to the whole phenomenon. The average person can't remember anything of their life before the age of three, but these "abductees" tend to demonstrate remarkable recall even to the point of birth. This leaves us with two options. Either their imagination is so active and the images so vivid that they cannot distinguish fact from fantasy, or their facility to see beyond everyday reality has made it possible for them to periodically perceive other dimensions and their inhabitants. It is a mistake to envisage this exchange in three-dimensional terms. We are not being probed by aliens from 'up there,' but from worlds that interpenetrate our own.

"There is overwhelming evidence that these experiences are not of a physical nature, but are a form of psychic communication between the individuals and other intelligences who are not necessarily alien. The reason that these contacts have been interpreted as being 'close encounters' with extraterrestrial life-forms is that our minds and our culture can only interpret them in terms of our experience. You only have to compare the way the technologically primitive people of the Pacific islands described their first sight of an aeroplane as being 'a big bird' to understand how the whole abduction phenomenon is a creation of our culture. At this moment in our evolution we have no way of accurately conveying the quality of these communications other than by using stereotypes and fantasy figures.

"After more than 25 years of research into the subject it is my opinion that these alleged encounters with aliens should be approached as dream-like experiences whose images are symbolic. It is highly significant that descriptions of the aliens fall into two distinct categories. One type is described as being small, ugly and squat just like the goblins of our fairy tales and the other is spoken of as being tall, extremely gifted and spiritually advanced like magicians or angels. Either these are archetypes from the unconscious mind, or interdimensional entities who individuals see in these forms because our culture has conditioned us to picture them as such. Those who are not so aware of their own latent psychic abilities and have no experience of paranormal phenomena are inclined to imagine that what they have sensed or seen with the inner eye are extraterrestrials. They don't understand the implications of what they have seen and so they fool themselves into thinking that it must be something unearthly because it is so different from the familiar, physical reality."

If that is indeed the case, then can we assume that Area 51, the ubiquitous Men in Black and all the other alien enthusiasts' obsessions are also unconscious projections of a certain paranoia and fear of the unknown?

"Area 51 exists. That's a fact. I have been there, but there are no captured UFOs there or alien bodies. Intelligence agencies are delighted that the UFO enthusiasts have given them this shroud of mystery because it camouflages what they are really up to: testing super-secret air-craft. The public are now so confused about what is really going on and so fearful of a possible alien invasion that they have stopped questioning the military about the destructive machines that it is making and the money that is being spent on these top-secret projects. The military doesn't even need to waste time creating misinformation as the UFO enthusiasts are doing it instead! If the whole alien abduction experience teaches us anything it should be that we need to spend more time exploring inner space and less time gazing into outer space in search of all the answers."

THE NEW MYTHOLOGY

IT APPEARS THAT the majority of abductees have inter-preted an inexplicable experience such as astral travel in terms of an abduction by aliens because they are unable to evaluate paranormal phenomena in any other way, and because alien images have become the symbolic language of our age. In the ancient world the earliest civilisations of Babylon, Sumeria and Egypt expressed their limited understanding of these unseen forces in terms of a universe dominated by gods and demons. In the Classical world these forces were personified in a whole pantheon of gods whose triumphs and struggles were immortalised in mythology. In biblical times, mystical glimpses of a greater reality and encounters with discarnate beings which inhabited the non-physical dimensions were described in terms of fiery chariots and angels in idealised human form. While in the Middle Ages many people believed in dragons, giants and demons because they suspected, and feared, that there was more to existence than mundane reality.

From the beginning, human beings have had a need to believe in a reality greater than their own; something which fires their imagination and relieves the boredom of the routine nature of daily life. It is our continuing fear of, and fascination with, the unknown which is the significant factor and not the form that it assumes.

WORLDS WITHIN WORLDS

THE SPIRITUAL ASPECT of the alien phenomenon was illuminated by the writer and mystic Paul Roberts. In an article for *Why* magazine in 1997, he described a meeting he had with the Indian guru Sai Baba which Roberts believed revealed the nature of the interdimensional intelligences with which an increasing number of people appear to be communicating. Baba is known as the "man of miracles" because of his reputed ability to heal the sick and to cause sacred ash known as "vibhuti" to materialise on his photographs owned by his 50 million devotees around the world.

Roberts asked Baba about life on other planets and was given a vision of the interpenetrating worlds in which we exist but of which our conscious minds are unaware. Baba asked Roberts to close his eyes and then he placed his thumb on the "third eye" in the centre of his forehead. As a more spiritually developed individual Baba is said to be able to raise the awareness of anyone who asks for insight simply by stimulating their third eye. "I saw world after jewelled world in a limitless cosmos of coiling self-illuminated spheres within spheres," Roberts recalled. "I was in each world simultaneously . . . their every inhabitant me and yet, also not me."

Roberts likened it to a dream in which everything he saw was a projection of himself; a creation of his mind which was also part of the Universal Mind. In that timeless moment he experienced the unity of existence and yet also appreciated its unique individuality. The universe was infinite, an ocean of worlds without end each teeming with a limitless variety of life. Baba brought him back with the words: "Outer space, inner space. Inner space the only real space . . . all things are really made by you, but for now you are thinking that God is making the grandeur of this universe."

ALTHOUGH EXTENSIVE SCIENTIFIC investigation by the world's space agencies has concluded that there are no advanced life-forms in our own solar system due to the inhospitable conditions on our neighbouring planets, it is inconceivable that there could be no other form of life elsewhere in the universe given the countless number of stars. Whether these life-forms are conscious, sentient beings with intelligence and the capability to transport themselves physically or otherwise through space is impossible to say for certain. However, the number of reported contacts by credible witnesses and the amount of photographic evidence that we have indicates that some form of communication is being attempted, although it is surely wishful thinking to imagine that they find us interesting enough to travel light years to examine us in such numbers night after night. Unfortunately, our need to believe that we are not alone in the universe, our growing distrust of governments and our capacity for self-deception combine to confuse the issue so that it has become almost impossible to distinguish genuine experiences from the specious.

Despite its technological achievements human nature has changed little since the invention of the wheel. People still fear the dark and look up in wonder at the night sky, although we have developed the technology needed to dispel the darkness and are better informed about our solar system. We have acquired a considerable amount of knowledge, but we have comparatively little understanding of the nature and purpose of our existence and seem no wiser than our ancestors on this point, judging by the violent events which characterised the 20th century.

For those searching for something that will give meaning and purpose to their lives, a belief in extraterrestrial life provides a certain stimulus, encouraging aspirations and justifying irrational fears.

I suggest that the UFO mystery reveals more about our need to be valued and considered interesting as individuals, and our hope for instant enlightenment to reveal the meaning of life than it does about extraterrestrial lifeforms.

It would seem that in spite of our technological advances we have not yet grown out of the need to believe in the gods.

PART THREE

STRANGE EXPERIMENTS

The extraordinary inventions of Nikola Tesla are not to be found in academic textbooks, nor will you find details of the U.S. navy's alleged time travel experiments during the 1940s in mainstream publications. However, all of these secret projects have been well documented in the "underground" specialist press and have been the subject of several bestsellers and television documentaries. Why? Is it because there is a worldwide conspiracy to conceal the truth from the public, or could it be that there is simply nothing substantial or conclusive to record?

14

NIKOLA TESLA

TO THE BEMUSED residents of Colorado Springs near Denver it must have seemed like a scene from a Frankenstein film. Their neighbour, Dr. Nikola Tesla, the eccentric but inspired Croatian-born inventor, was creating a violent electrical storm in his laboratory one cloudless evening in 1899, the crackle of the giant coils echoing across the eerily deserted streets. Dr. Tesla had previously proved the power of his wireless electrical transmitter/receiver by illuminating 200 bulbs at a distance of 40 kilometres, but this latest demonstration was far more ambitious. He hoped to send a stream of increasingly powerful electrical pulses around the world which his 60-metre high mast would receive on its return, before sending out another of even greater strength until he had created a cycle of electrical waves. The theory was based on his belief that the earth is a natural conductor and that a strategically placed grid of these masts fed by a number of hydroelectric plants could be used to supply free electricity to people around

the world. All they would need would be a small trans-
former which would pick up the current from a metal rod
planted in their back yard and relay it to antennae fixed to
their electrical appliances.

As the bewildered Colorado Springs residents peered
from behind their curtains that auspicious evening, a surge
of electrical current arced into the sky, growing in intensity
until it had reached 50 metres up in the air. The surge created a static discharge which illuminated the earth, sending
insects hot-footing across the eerily glowing grass and
sparks crackling beneath the shoes of anyone who had
ventured outside. Only Dr. Tesla was isolated from the
effects. He had avoided singeing his shoes by wearing rubber soles. The eerie illuminations finally ended when the
voltage became so great that it melted the city's generator.
Dr. Tesla's experiments may sound like the exploits of
another crackpot inventor, but there are those who believe
that we have good reason to take him and his radical ideas
very seriously indeed.

EARLY INVENTIONS

TESLA WAS BORN in Croatia in 1856 but quickly rose
above his humble origins by teaching himself a staggering
six languages and demonstrating an intuitive understanding of science which was beyond that of his teachers. It is
said that he possessed a photographic memory and was a
mathematical prodigy, but his most remarkable talent was
his ability to visualise his inventions in the minutest detail
in the form of a mental blueprint so that when they were
eventually built—sometimes many years later—nothing
had been left to chance. One of his earliest ideas was for

an "induction" motor powered by rotating magnetic fields which has since become a basic component of every fridge and washing machine to roll off the assembly line, but Tesla is not credited with its invention. His plans were dismissed at the time as being too fanciful.

At the age of 28, with little prospect of funding or commercial success in Eastern Europe, Tesla emigrated to America where he found employment with Thomas Edison. Although Edison is customarily credited with over a thousand inventions, most notably the phonograph and the incandescent electric lamp, it now appears that he was a shrewd businessman who allegedly picked the brains of his more innovative apprentices and claimed their innovations as his own. Tesla supporters, who actively campaign to have his genius officially recognised, maintain that Edison refused to credit the Croatian's innovations or pay him royalties which were due under a "gentleman's agreement." Others insist that Tesla was so disgusted with the American's business methods that he tore up the royalty contracts which would have made him a multi-millionaire and he refused to share the Nobel Prize in Physics which they had been awarded jointly in 1912.

It is also believed that Edison belittled Tesla's hope that alternating current (a continuous electric current that periodically reverses direction) could provide affordable electricity for everyone, and that Edison went to extraordinary lengths to promote a more expensive and less reliable system using direct current (a continuous electric current that flows in one direction only without a sizeable variation in magnitude). It is generally assumed that Edison took this unusual course either because he was intensely defensive of his own reputation, and having stated an opinion he

found it impossible to retract it, or because he had a vested
interest in the commercial use of direct current.

In public Edison claimed that alternating current was
not only unreliable, but lethal, and to prove it he used it
to electrocute puppies before an invited audience. Subsequent demonstrations witnessed the deaths of more
helpless animals, including an elephant, until the New
York prison authorities declared themselves convinced
of its lethal potential and commissioned the building of
the first electric chair for the execution of convicted
criminals.

TESLA'S TV TRANSMITTER

A DECADE BEFORE Marconi made his historic transat-
lantic radio transmissions in December 1900, Tesla had
announced plans for a global grid of transmission towers
and receivers which could broadcast both pictures and
sound across the airwaves. It has been suggested by Tesla's
disciples that a similar grid system of pyramids and
obelisks had been used to broadcast energy in both ancient
Egypt and the lost continent of Atlantis, and that Tesla was,
in effect, reinventing devices using technology which had
been known to the ancients.

Unlikely though it might seem, he may have gained
this, and other, knowledge by psychically searching what
is known as the Akashic Records, or "world memory"
which the thoughts of generations have impressed upon
the ether. A number of celebrated sensitives have used this
method to make a string of uncannily accurate predictions,
such as the American prophet and healer Edgar Cayce who
regularly accessed this living archive in order to prescribe

cures of which he had no conscious knowledge. Whether or not Tesla did probe the past in this way it is impossible to say, but he is known to have practised a form of visualisation on a regular basis which sounds similar to remote viewing.

"I saw new scenes. These were at first blurred and indistinct and would flit away when I tried to concentrate my attention on them. They gained strength and distinctness and finally assumed the concreteness of real things ... Every night, and sometimes during the day ... I would start on my journeys, see new places, cities and countries ..."

With $150,000 in funding from financier J. P. Morgan, Tesla built his first broadcasting tower on Long Island in New York state, but as this monument to his genius rose skyward like a modern tower of Babel, Tesla's visions became more and more fanciful. He claimed that the transmitter could generate 100 billion watts which could be focused in the form of a death ray to direct a destructive force equivalent to ten megatonnes of TNT anywhere in the world. Morgan refused to fund any more projects and other backers were not forthcoming. As the debts mounted, Tesla suffered a nervous breakdown and was forced to sell the laboratory at Colorado Springs, much to the relief of the residents. He also closed the transmitter at Long Island although it remained operational. This fact was not lost on the tabloid press who, in 1907, speculated that Tesla's death ray may have been responsible for the mysterious sinking of the French ship *Iena*, which accounts say "exploded under mysterious circumstances," reminding readers of its inventor's boast that the device could ignite a ship's magazine and send it to the bottom in a matter of minutes. When questioned, Tesla became uncharacteristically silent on the subject, though a year later he admitted to a reporter that wireless plants of this type could render an entire region uninhabitable at the flick of a switch.

There has recently also been speculation that Tesla's death ray caused the massive explosion at Tunguska in central Siberia on the morning of 30 June 1908 which incinerated 200,000 hectares of forest without leaving a crater of any kind and which has never been satisfactorily explained. But if he had wanted to prove the destructive capacity of his device surely it would have been more effective to level a disused factory or melt a monument in Central Park? Although it sounds like the stuff of science fiction, the death ray and Tesla's detailed plans for particle beam weapons became the foundation and principle of the Star Wars space weapons project in the 1980s.

In recognition of his pioneering work Tesla was subsequently granted the fundamental radio patent by the U.S. Supreme Court, but he died before he could claim his share of the profits. Since his death in 1943 the true extent of his prodigious imagination has become known, although it is unlikely that more than a few of his 1,200 patents would have proven practical. There was little chance of his anti-gravity airships taking to the skies, no practical application for his legendary earthquake machine and commercial interests would never have allowed the development of free energy devices. In fact, there may be some substance in the suspicion that U.S. government agencies suppressed news of his inventions. After his death his plans and papers were confiscated and shortly afterwards his laboratory was burnt to the ground. When the papers were eventually returned after much petitioning of officials by his family, all mention of his secret weapons projects had been removed.

15

THE PHILADELPHIA EXPERIMENT

IN THE 1984 science fiction film *The Philadelphia Experiment* an American sailor serving on a wartime destroyer is projected 40 years into the future and several members of the crew are injured or driven insane when a radar invisibility test goes badly wrong. The authors of the book on which the film was based, William Moore and Charles Berlitz, claimed that the story was based on a real incident which took place at the Philadelphia Naval Yard in 1943, but neither they nor a succession of independent investigators were able to provide firm evidence.

Although the whole episode sounds implausible in the extreme there are a number of curious elements which suggest that something strange and highly secret was being tested in the area at that time and that witnesses may have been silenced to prevent the truth from being told.

Details of the incident first came to light in the spring

of 1956 when Dr. Morris K. Jessup, a distinguished American scientist and teacher of astronomy and mathematics at the University of Michigan, received a number of letters from a source who signed as Carl M. Allen. Allen, who later revealed his real name to be Carlos Allende, claims to have been a crew member aboard the liberty ship SS *Furuseth* berthed at the Norfolk Portsmouth base and to have seen some early, similar experiments which took place at sea. Based on what he saw at Norfolk, he alleged that the navy had developed a device for making ships invisible to enemy radar using Einstein's unified field theory. Jessup had apparently impressed Allende with his discussion of the practical applications of Einstein's theory in his book *The Case for the UFO*—one of the first serious studies of the phenomenon—along with the case for the existence of anti-gravity devices which could facilitate space travel.

The unified field theory would have described the properties of gravitational and electromagnetic fields, and nuclear interactions in one equation, just as the formula $E=MC^2$ conveyed the concept of relativity. But Einstein did not publish the results of his calculations and it has been assumed that he was unable to formulate his theory. However, Allende claims that the great scientist had succeeded, but soon afterwards he realised to what destructive and manipulative uses it could be put and he destroyed his notes. Before he did so he entrusted his discovery to a Dr. B. Russell who allegedly passed it on to Dr. Franklin Reno of the top-secret Naval Research and Development Unit.

During the early years of World War II Dr. Reno is said to have worked on the initial experiments for what was officially designated Project Invisibility, a top-secret weapons project overseen by Rear Admiral Rawson Bennett. Bennett was then Navy Chief of Research and presumably one of the few officials who could verify what actually happened at the base in 1943, but by all accounts he has maintained a strict silence on the subject. What we do know following the investigations made by Dr. Jessup, William Moore and Charles Berlitz is that for these early tests several powerful magnetic generators, known as degaussers, were used to create a resonatic magnetic field around objects which would effectively be isolated in a fifth dimension. The aim was to develop a portable device with which all military ships, planes and tanks would be equipped that would render them invisible to enemy radar, but the team failed to anticipate the side-effects of the force field. When the USS *Eldridge* was equipped with the modified generators in October 1943 it underwent a series of tests at an isolated dock at the naval base and also at sea. During one of these, the intense magnetic field is said to have caused the ship to disappear physically as well as on the radar screens and reappear 200 miles away at the Norfolk Portsmouth naval base where it was usually berthed, though perhaps as a holographic image rather than in physical form. A few moments later it reappeared at the Philadelphia dock showing no signs of structural damage, but manned by a crew who were exhibiting serious psychological disorders.

Because of the top-secret nature of the tests and the wartime restrictions which forbade military personnel from speaking openly of such things, there is a serious shortage of reliable witnesses. Allende is one of the few to have come forward. Another is Al Bielek who claims to have been an officer aboard the *Eldridge* during the tests which he alleges projected him and his brother Duncan 40 years into the future. Bielek has recorded his experiences

in a book entitled *The Philadelphia Experiment* and on a
series of videos in which he also talks about US government time travel experiments at the Montauk Point Military Base near New York and their development of Dr.
Tesla's death ray. But the more outrageous his claims
became the less credible a witness he seemed.

Allende's testimony was also suspect. Inconsistencies
in his letters to Dr. Jessup suggested that he too was an
unreliable witness. Allende claimed to have read a report
of the incident in a Philadelphia newspaper, as if to
confirm his story, but no such report was published at the
time. Moreover, in his letters Allende initially describes
the experiment as having taken place in Philadelphia (presumably meaning on the Delaware River), but he later
writes of it taking place at sea. His descriptions of his time
travel experiences and of the role played by alien technology appear increasingly preposterous. However, after Dr.
Jessup began making discreet inquiries into the incident he
was invited to appear at the Office of Naval Research and
was questioned about his relationship with Allende. During the interview he was shown a heavily annotated copy
of *The Case for the UFO* and asked to compare the hand-
writing in the margins with the Allende letters which he
had brought with him. There was little doubt that the notes
in the book and the letters had been written by the same
person. Consequently, Dr. Jessup was persuaded to part
with the letters on the grounds that they might constitute
evidence of treason and that failure on his part to hand
them over could be perceived as complicity to disclose
military secrets. Soon after, Allende mysteriously disappeared from his home in New Kensington, Pennsylvania
and was never seen alive again.

Dr. Jessup was subsequently offered a senior post at the

Office of Naval Research, ostensibly to work on similar projects to the Philadelphia Experiment, but he turned it down because he feared that the projected devices were potentially more dangerous than the atomic bomb. He has been quoted as saying:

> "This use of magnetic resonance is tantamount to temporary obliteration in our dimensions, but it tends to get out of control. Actually it is equivalent to transference of matter into another level, or dimension, and could represent a dimensional breakthrough if it were possible to control it."

As any competent mathematician will confirm, abstract mathematics allows for the existence of 26 dimensions in addition to the four of the physical world, although, in theory, an infinite number are possible. And if these dimensions are possible in theory then the laws of mathematics state that they ought to exist in fact.

This concept has been expanded upon by Dr. Manson Valentine, a colleague and close friend of Dr. Jessup, who gave an explanation during an interview with Charles Berlitz. Berlitz was then working on a book concerning the mysterious disappearances of numerous ships and planes in the Bermuda Triangle, an area of the Atlantic Ocean which is bounded by Bermuda, Puerto Rico and Florida. The inference was that the devices used in the Philadelphia Experiment may have replicated a natural atmospheric phenomenon which had claimed the planes and ships which disappeared in the Atlantic.

Dr. Valentine attempted to explain how such dematerialisations are possible by remarking that many scientists now believe that basic atomic structure is essentially elec-

trical energy rather than physical particles. He described
the universe as being composed of "multiple phases of
matter" bound together by a vast interplay of energies
which means that space and time are not absolutes but are
more flexible, dependent upon one's perspective. Dr.
Valentine explained:

> "The transition from one phase to another would be
> equivalent to the passage from one plane of existence to
> another—a sort of interdimensional metamorphosis. In
> other words, there could be worlds within worlds."

Curiously, this is the vision of mystics through the ages
who claim to have glimpsed a "greater reality" beyond our
three-dimensional world of matter (see page 133). He
added:

> "Whenever we encounter incredible [to us] materialisa-
> tion and dematerialisation, as in UFO phenomena, they
> seem to be accompanied by severe magnetic distur-
> bances. It is therefore reasonable to suppose that a pur-
> poseful genesis of unusual magnetic conditions could
> effect a change of phase in matter, both physical and
> vital. If so, it would also distort the time element which
> is by no means an independent entity, but part of a par-
> ticular matter–energy–time dimension such as the one
> we live in."

Unfortunately, neither Berlitz nor his co-author William
Moore were able to interview Dr. Jessup for on 20 April
1959 the scientist was found dead in his car after inhaling
carbon-monoxide fed from the exhaust. The coroner's verdict was suicide, but the conspiracy theorists contend that

he signed his own death warrant when he handed over the Allende letters.

THE RUSSIAN VERSION

AN INTERESTING POSTSCRIPT was added by the writer Robert Charroux who extracted the following information from the Romanian scientist Doru Todericiu. According to Todericiu, the Russians were treating seriously rumours that the American navy had been experimenting during the war with radar invisibility using a submarine, not a destroyer, and that they had succeeded in transporting the sub from the Philadelphia dock to Norfolk, as Allende had claimed.

The principle involved was again a magnetic field, but in the form of a moebius strip, which is a one-sided geometrical figure which one can make by twisting a strip of paper and then joining the ends together. If a line is drawn down the centre it will form a continuous circle without having to change sides and yet, when the circle is cut along the line, it will form a large ring and not two smaller circles as logic suggests. In the experiment the American submarine is said to have created a moebius strip by turning over once during each circuit then severing the magnetic field it had created with the onboard electronics. Unfortunately, Todericiu was unable to discover if the Russians had embarked on a similar series of experiments and if so, whether or not they had succeeded in penetrating the fifth dimension.

THE NOTORIOUS MAGICIAN Aleister Crowley once admitted that he had put just enough "chocolate" in his magical recipes to make them taste like chocolate cake, by which he meant that he had divulged just enough information to make his books convincing, but not so much that he had given away all his secrets. The Philadelphia Experiment and the curious case of Nikola Tesla both contain just enough verifiable facts to sound convincing and yet both leave many fundamental questions unanswered.

Some researchers have expressed doubts that the Philadelphia Experiment ever took place and claim that Dr. Jessup's death was, in fact, suicide. He is known to have been depressed by his failure as a writer, and his plans for further research into the UFO phenomenon had been frustrated. The inconsistencies in the Allende letters and the increasingly outrageous claims by "survivor" Al Bielek cast more doubts on the whole subject and yet U.S. naval intelligence was evidently eager to keep something under wraps.

The case of Nikola Tesla is another curious amalgam of facts and speculation. We are asked to believe that the U.S. government conspired with "commercial interests" to suppress Tesla's plans for free electricity, plans which have never been proven to be practical. In fact, Tesla's extraordinary claims concerning his death ray and his subsequent eccentric behaviour suggest that he was not to be taken seriously in the first instance, although he no doubt possessed a remarkable mathematical mind and imagination. Is it not more likely then that his papers were confiscated following his death in 1943 because America was at war and the government did not want to risk designs for a death ray, no matter how implausible, falling into the wrong hands?

Truth may be stranger than fiction, but we seem to prefer the myth to the mundane because it is infinitely more interesting.

16

REMOTE VIEWING AND AMERICA'S PSYCHIC SPIES

OF ALL MY many psychic experiences the most inexplicable remains my first encounter with the phenomenon known as remote viewing.

Many years ago I attended a psychic awareness group near my home in Kent led by a woman to whom I readily admitted that I had not had the quality of visions which other members had been describing, whereupon she offered to give me a "helping hand." With a knowing smile she crossed over to where I was sitting and placed her hand at the base of my spine. Then she asked me to close my eyes and describe what I saw. After a few moments I had the image of my own living room but with several significant details superimposed on the main picture. As I began to describe aloud what I was seeing my own home faded and the unfamiliar furniture and surroundings came into sharper focus. I was able to describe in great detail this other home and extend my view to the garden where I noticed a curious feature, a statue of Eros which did not seem to belong. It was in focus, but it was at an odd angle. When I had finished I was coolly informed that I had been describing an apartment belonging to the woman's mother in New York! The statue of Eros was explained by the fact that they had recently been talking about meeting at Piccadilly Circus on the mother's next visit to England.

I have no explanation as to how I was able to tune in to a location that meant nothing to me, nor how the woman's thoughts managed to impress themselves upon my mind other than by accepting the possibility that it was a form of mental telepathy or assisted remote viewing. Neither do I believe that she told me I had seen the New York apartment simply to impress me as she could have gained nothing from having done so. She was not even being paid to hold the meeting.

TESTING THE BOUNDARIES

REMOTE VIEWING INVOLVES a projection of consciousness to a distant location and is often confused with an out-of-body experience, but it is quite unique and not as rare as one might imagine. Since the 1970s several celebrated psychics have subjected themselves to experiments to test the validity of the technique under stringent laboratory conditions, which led both the CIA and the KGB to train psychic spies in remote viewing techniques for their paranormal espionage programmes.

Of the former, the most convincing "subject" was the New York sensitive Ingo Swann who in the 1970s submitted to an exhaustive series of tests under the supervision of physicist and parapsychologist Dr. H. Puthoff and physicist Russell Targ for the American Society for Psychical Research at Stanford Research Institute (SRI) in California.

Swann had initially been asked to psychically scan the contents of sealed envelopes, but he soon became bored and challenged the scientists to find a more demanding test for his talents. It was his idea to then experiment with a technique that he called "remote viewing," which at first involved projecting his consciousness to a platform suspended from the laboratory ceiling on which had been placed geometrical shapes. But after correctly identifying and drawing these repeatedly either by clairvoyance, telepathy or out-of-body vision Swann again grew restless and suggested that he be given random latitudinal and longitudinal co-ordinates of a target location anywhere in the world that he could probe by psychic means.

Of 100 separate tests he was able to supply accurate and detailed descriptions for 43 of the locations which were subsequently verified and 32 descriptions which were correct in many respects. On one memorable occasion he supplied the scientists with a detailed drawing of an island in the Indian Ocean showing key features including a landing field, jetty, boats and a lighthouse. Although at the time the research team insisted that there was nothing at that location, subsequent research verified what Swann had seen.

His success soon attracted the attention of the CIA who allegedly gave the SRI team a $50,000 grant to find a "repeatable phenomenon" that could have intelligence-gathering applications. As an acid test a CIA representative gave Swann and his new partner, retired police commissioner Pat Price, the co-ordinates of a friend's holiday cabin near Washington on the other side of the U.S. which no one at Stanford could have known about. But the co-ordinates were slightly inaccurate and the two psychics homed in on a neighbouring secret military installation instead. The details that they were able to give the incredulous government agent included the names of personnel who were working at the base and the code words for the secret files that were stored there in locked cabinets. These details were sufficient to convince the Pentagon to fund the psychic spy programme that was to become known as Stargate.

CONFESSIONS OF A PSYCHIC SPY

ONE OF THE first recruits to the unit was an American army major called David Morehouse who claims to have revealed the inside story of the unit's missions and methods in his international bestseller, *Psychic Warrior*.

It all began when this self-confessed career soldier, distinguished military graduate and highly decorated U.S. army officer with no interest in the paranormal was accidentally shot in the head during a training exercise in the spring of 1987. The bullet lodged in David's helmet, knocking him unconscious and sending him into the "twilight zone." In the months following his recovery he started to have disturbing out-of-body experiences and began to doubt his own sanity. Then, just as he was seriously considering resigning his commission on health grounds, he was persuaded to transfer to the Defense Department to train as a psychic spy for Stargate. There, at a secret base at Fort Meade, he discovered that his extrasensory abilities were far from unique. He was just one of several ex-military personnel to have been recruited.

Each remote viewing trip followed a set pattern. In a designated room at Stargate HQ, David would make himself comfortable on a specially designed bed called the viewing platform and dim the lights to create the right atmosphere. Facing him would sit a "monitor," another member of the team who ran the video cameras and tape machines which recorded every detail of the mission. It was the monitor who read out the co-ordinates of the chosen target—the nature of which was always unknown to the viewers until after their debriefing. With the co-ordinates fixed in his mind the viewer then entered an altered state of consciousness similar to that attained in deep meditation, before projecting their "phantom body," as David calls it, into the ether.

The separation from the physical body always began with a sound like ripping Velcro and then the viewers found themselves suspended in the darkness of space gazing down on planet earth. Moments later they descended through a tunnel at increasing speed with the surrounding stars blurring into streaks of light until their phantom body struck a membrane-like substance which indicated that they had hit the target area. David admits that he still doesn't understand exactly how it works, his only concern had been to "brace himself for the ride" and describe as accurately as he could what he saw when he got there.

Surprisingly, he doesn't accept that what he experienced was a form of astral projection.

"An out-of-body experience is a completely different phenomenon. Remote viewing does not require the subject to leave the body. It is a projection of consciousness involving the opening of conduits into the time–space continuum. Out-of-body experiences tend to be rare,

unprompted excursions by the astral body or to a particular plane of existence in sympathy with its vibrational
rate. Remote viewing projects the consciousness at will
anywhere in the ether and only after a prolonged period
of intense training.

"Of course everything you get during remote viewing
is filtered through the conscious mind which interprets
the images, smells, tastes and emotional impressions as
conditioned by the viewer's own previous experiences. So
we were trained to be able to differentiate between what
was really out there and what was stimulated by our
imagination. They cautioned us against what they called
'analytical overlay,' that is, the intrusion of the conscious
mind to automatically kick in and analyse something it
doesn't recognise. Much of what is in the ether does not
fit into everyday experience so the conscious mind can't
compute it, so to speak. It therefore adds lots of other data
from its own memory so that we can accept it as 'real.'
Even with us, it still crept in and coloured the raw data.
For that reason remote viewing is never 100 per cent accurate. Anyone who tells you it is, is lying!"

David explains in his book that sometimes the target would
be a secret and inaccessible military installation far into
enemy territory, a nuclear sub in the middle of the ocean,
or even a test pilot in flight. Occasionally the viewers were
sent unknowingly to sites such as the Auschwitz concentration camp to acclimatise their newfound senses to "negative energies."

When experiencing such disturbing trips did David
actually believe at the time that he was in danger, or was
he just hypersensitive to negative energies?

"Good question. I was probably just hypersensitive. I wasn't aware of any overtly negative force in the ether exerting its influence on me or any of the other viewers, but there is a cumulative effect from being exposed to so much negative energy or emotion which some of us felt. You have to remember that the targets were not chosen to be an enlightening experience. We were systematically exposed to violent or negative incidents and locations such as the ovens at Auschwitz and the destruction of the 103 Airbus over Lockerbie for the purpose of sensitising ourselves to these vibrations so that we would recognise them when we were sent in to sense the reactions of a Soviet test pilot, for example. After having been exposed to great waves of distress and fear at Auschwitz, for example, we would then be able to recognise the sensations present at a secret police headquarters or forced labour camp, or pick up more sensitive vibrations such as irritation from the test pilot which might tell us that he is experiencing insufficient power during a climb, or whatever. It's the same thing that happens to the physical body after suffering from frostbite. The next time the body senses cold anywhere below what it considers to be normal, it manifests psychosomatic symptoms of frostbite. And that's also what happens with extremely intense emotional energies.

"But I must point out that whenever we 'returned' from a mission, our data was collated with information taken from many other sources including satellite scans, photos and human reconnaissance and sent for analysis. The fact remains that remote viewing is not 100 per cent accurate and it never will be. You can never rely exclusively on a single operative, despite what the guys now offering expensive courses will tell you. Remote viewing is not a stand-alone endeavour. No mission was ever sanctioned solely on the information gained from remote viewing. It was only one piece of the puzzle. Initially the top brass said that if it proved to be only 5 per cent accurate then it would be of value, but I know it has often proved to run at around 80 per cent accuracy and sometimes even more."

At the time of his induction into the unit was he aware that the Soviets had a similar programme in operation?

"Yes. Knowledge of the Soviet's activities is what actually prompted the U.S. to set up its own remote viewing programme. And then shortly afterwards we discovered that the Czechs, Chinese, British and Israelis also had similar programmes. And they are all still active today. They were all pretty much equal as far as their achievements and potential went, except for the Soviets who were well ahead of the others for the simple fact that they could call on 'naturals' from the population at large. If the Russians heard that some peasant worker had been run over by a truck and developed ESP as a side-effect, for example, their intelligence people could simply drive out to his home and forcibly conscript him into the service. We had to wait until someone in the forces developed something and then we had to persuade them to subject themselves to training.

"But the Soviets soon found that their people began breaking away as the state lost its grip on them. I know for a fact that their best-known psychic spy, Ivan Sokalov, offered his services to the global corporate market and the rumour is that he has been snapped up by a multinational consumer electronics company. Some of my colleagues dispute this, but then I ask them to tell me where he is and who is paying his salary!"

From the descriptions of his training and experiences David appears to have been excited rather than apprehensive at the prospect of exploring the unknown. So, is there nothing, in his experience, to fear out there?

"When the veil is drawn back and other dimensions are revealed there are a great many things to fear, although mostly it's the inability to digest the enormity of this greater reality. Certainly there are other worlds, peoples and dimensions—many of them benign and a great many of them malevolent—but there is, to the best of my knowledge and experience, no single dark force out there.

"I encountered what I call lesser beings or demons on several occasions. They look just like us and appear friendly until you realise what they are. Then they use your fears against you. They can sense what scares you because they exist in the realm of the emotions which is a level remote viewers often explore. What really scared me was sensing their hunger to take me over and possess my body. But I also encountered benign, enlightened beings, such as my own personal guardian angel and others who had the Christ consciousness. Unfortunately, they seemed to regard us as harmless intruders and refused to interact with us."

Did David ever get any insights into extraterrestrial life-forms during his trips into the ether?

"Yes. Certainly there is life out there. We are not alone, I know that. A great deal of rubbish has been written about UFOs, but as with all these things there is a certain amount of truth behind it.

"I couldn't tell you for sure that Area 51 is a secret base for crashed UFOs so I won't speculate as others have done. I don't want to compromise my credibility by speculating. I have only talked and written about what I have gleaned from direct personal experience.

"I have to laugh when I hear of so-called UFO specialists superimposing photos of secret military aircraft over what are alleged to be photos of UFOs and saying that the similarity of their outlines is categorical proof that the US government is appropriating extraterrestrial technology! When you ask these people where they get their information from they invariably claim to know someone inside Area 51, but those are the guys taking government pay cheques to dish out misinformation! They're laughing at these gullible idiots behind their backs. You shouldn't believe anything about Area 51 or these so-called secret bases unless you are personally led by the hand on a guided tour and see it for yourself.

"I can tell you three things about UFOs. One is that they exist. Two: the governments of the world know that they exist. And three: they don't want you to know that they know they exist. There is a lot of deception and damage control going on to make sure that what has leaked out is tricked up and camouflaged with a lot of nonsense that can be disputed or disproved."

The big question has got to be: is the truth really out there, or is it far more complex than that? Are there just different shades of grey?

"That's a very interesting question. No one has ever asked me that before. If I think about it I'd have to say that there appear to be many shades of the truth. What I describe in my book is one 'best' version of it, if you can accept that description. There doesn't seem to be one indelible blueprint which tells you to turn right here and then left there. Whatever the great plan might be there is always free agency or free will in operation. Our future is determined by free will, not an act of God.

"The ability to discern the truth lies with that still, small voice within us which we can call instinct or intuition. Although remote viewing sounds as if it's something right out of the *X Files*, it really comes down to developing or fine-tuning the intuition which we all have. It's learning to open the conduits of our hidden senses which bleed over into the superconsciousness of which we are all a part. If you practise it you'll start to know things you can't have gleaned with the conscious mind and you won't know how you know them."

The claims made by David Morehouse have been corroborated on camera by a number of senior military personnel and my own experience of remote viewing has convinced me that a projection of consciousness such as that which he describes is possible, but the experience itself is highly subjective and the results are erratic. Morehouse admitted that the military never relied solely on information obtained by the remote viewing unit and he has expressed doubts about the claims made by those individuals who are now offering courses on the subject.

PART FOUR

PARANORMAL PUZZLES

During my childhood I periodically had out-of-body experiences during which I was fully conscious and aware that what I was experiencing was quite distinct from a dream. I had the sensation of floating free of my body, of exploring my surroundings from a new, bird's-eye perspective. I crossed oceans and unfamiliar landscapes to visit relatives who were unaware of my presence before I returned to my sleeping body with a familiar falling sensation. As an adult my astral travels became more infrequent, although I still occasionally wake from a dream to find myself in another part of the house before being snapped back into my body, or drift in and out of my body as I consider whether to go on another "trip" or go back to sleep.

There is nothing unique in this ability. We all do it, only we tend to dismiss it as a dream, either because we simply don't believe that such things are possible, or because subsequent dreams obscure the reality of what we have experienced by the time we awake. The result of these astral excursions was to convince me that what we imagine to be supernatural powers are simply an acute awareness of this greater reality which is normally limited by our physical senses. In the following pages I hope to show that psychic abilities are something that we can all cultivate and that having nurtured this facility we will lose our obsession with the transitory things of the material world, and with it our fear of the unknown.

17

PSYCHIC PHENOMENA—THE GIFT OF SECOND SIGHT?

A SENSATION-SEEKING media are largely to blame for creating the myth that psychic power is an exceptional gift which is randomly bestowed upon unsuspecting individuals who ultimately discover that "knowing too much" can be a curse rather than a blessing. In the real world psychics tend to be very ordinary people who come to accept their insights as simply a heightened sensitivity to impressions in the ether and auras given off by every individual. For that reason they frequently prefer to be known as sensitives, or intuitives rather than psychics or mediums. Mediums are traditionally those who specialise in making contact with the discarnate spirits of the deceased, but in all psychic work, the subtle—if sometimes overpowering—vibrations that psychics sense create impressions in the mind which must be distinguished from the creations of the individual's own unconscious.

In a recent Gallup survey conducted in Britain 50 per cent of those questioned believed that they had experienced some form of psychic insight. It is thought that we all share these latent talents, but most of us ignore the small voice within that is our "higher self" and dismiss our hunches because we have been conditioned to distrust our intuition. Instead we sleepwalk through a world of infinite interest which we perceive as if blinkered simply because we have been taught that intuition is a redundant primitive instinct and the products of our imagination are unreal. Psychic experience suggests otherwise; that imagination is the facility through which we can glimpse a greater reality—the world of spirit.

PSYCHIC RESEARCH

WHILST THE SCIENTIFIC establishment remains stubbornly sceptical with regard to all aspects of paranormal phenomena the evidence in favour of its existence is considerable. In the 1930s Dr. J. B. Rhine, who is generally considered to be the father of experimental parapsychology, conducted a comprehensive series of tests over an eight-year period drawing upon students from Duke University in North Carolina as his subjects.

Using a pack of five specially designed cards, each with a simple shape or figure, he demonstrated that some of the students were able to guess correctly which card he was holding more often than could be attributed to mere chance. He named this talent extra sensory perception or ESP.

Dr. Rhine also investigated a gambler's claim that he could influence the fall of dice and was sufficiently impressed to initiate a series of experiments in psychokinesis, or mind over matter, again using the Duke University students as subjects. Rhine found that they too could influence the fall of the dice, but only when their level of interest was high. Their success rate rapidly declined as the tests went on, regardless of how much they concentrated on their task, suggesting that psychic ability is sharpened by a certain, unspecified state of mind. But perhaps the most convincing demonstration of paranormal power was given by the psychic Ingo Swann during a series of tests devised by physicist and parapsychologist Harold Puthoff at Stanford Research Institute in California in the 1970s (see page 158). Puthoff had reservations regarding the results obtained by Rhine which he suspected might still contain an element of chance and so he designed a test which would eliminate this completely.

Puthoff believed that psychic energy is essentially magnetic and that a genuine psychic would be able to influence a magnetic field, the fluctuations of which could be recorded. To this end he enlisted the assistance of fellow physicist Arthur Hebard who had access to a highly sensitive magnetometer which is used for measuring magnetic fields. Swann was then challenged to alter the magnetic field of the core. This was shielded by four layers of material, including a supercooled electrical coil, and placed in an eight-tonne iron vault encased in concrete beneath the laboratory floor to isolate it from outside influences. Within minutes the waves traced by the instrument's recorder doubled in frequency as Swann probed the core, then the magnetic activity ceased entirely. After 45 seconds Swann announced that he could not hold it any longer and the recorder kicked into life again as the magnetic activity resumed.

As if to satisfy all doubts Swann then sketched the interior of the magnetometer showing features that he could not possibly have known were there, leaving the physicists to declare themselves more than satisfied that they now had conclusive proof of psychic ability.

THE HEALER'S EXPERIENCE

KARIN PAGE, FOUNDER of the Star of the East spiritual healing centre in Kent and a practising sensitive with a common-sense approach to the paranormal, defines psychic ability as a sensitivity to subtle energies, rather than a gift arbitrarily bestowed on chosen individuals by a benign creator.

> "I believe that we are all born with psychic ability. It is just that we have forgotten how to tap into that energy. It is usually awoken through experiences which force us to question the purpose of life, or it can be stimulated by meeting with spiritually aware people at the right time in our lives. They might get us to look at the world in a less materialistic way and perhaps encourage us to trust more in our intuition, which is the first step to psychic development.
>
> "My first psychic experience occurred spontaneously when I was six years old, although being so young I didn't realise that was what it was. I was gazing idly out of my bedroom window when I saw a couple walking arm in arm along the road and then suddenly they vanished like smoke. It might sound strange now, but being so young I just assumed it was nothing unusual and I wasn't frightened. I didn't think of them as spirits or ghosts, because

they looked so solid, so real. I just imagined that they were so in love that they had turned into trees or something like characters sometimes do in fairy tales."

Having a blank, receptive or open mind often seems to be the trigger for these glimpses into another dimension. Could it be that the ability to relax into a meditative state is all that distinguishes the psychic, or sensitive, from the sceptic?

"My own experiences and those of other mediums that I have met and worked with suggest that contact with spirit is a two-way process. Some mediums are born with a natural gift of 'second sight,' as they used to call it, but sometimes spirit will want to communicate with the living and if the individual is not open to receive the message then spirit might steer them into what appears to be a coincidental meeting with a medium so that the message can be passed on.

"The intuitive knowledge that these mediums possess comes from their own higher self and that is why there is nothing to fear about opening oneself up to higher knowledge. There seems to be a greater proportion of female mediums and that is simply because women tend to trust more in their intuition. But when men learn to do so they often become quite powerful healers."

Initially Karin's awareness of other levels of being expressed itself in subtle ways. During her teens and early 20s she would read about something which she felt she already knew, or of which she had a deeper understanding than could be accounted for by her education. Then, when she was 28 years old, she had an experience which convinced her of the existence of life after death and demonstrated to her beyond doubt that our physical world is only one form of reality.

"I had caught pneumonia and had been taken to hospital where I had a near-death experience which I shall never forget. It was more vivid and real than what we call real life. My mind was crystal clear and alert, not like in a dream where you find yourself in an imaginary landscape. I remember it was 6 o'clock in the morning, the time they brought the tea and coffee round the wards. I simply drifted out of my body up towards the ceiling and when I looked back I saw my body lying in the bed. At that moment the nurse came in and put a teacup next to my bed. Then she noticed that I was in trouble and called the doctor. I could see what was going on but I couldn't hear what they said. It was as if I had been cosseted in a warm, pure stillness. It was utter peace, bliss, joy, release. I wasn't concerned at all for the figure lying in the bed, it had nothing to do with the real me.

"Then I turned to the light above me which I sensed was beckoning me. Unlike sunlight I could look straight into this light without any problem. It was intense but not uncomfortable to look into. I couldn't see anything beyond the light. But I kept wanting to look back at the form on the bed and I remember thinking: 'What's all the fuss? Why are they fussing about it? I'm all right.' I wanted to go on into the light, but something was drawing me back. Then suddenly I was back in my body.

"For the next three hours I drifted in and out of consciousness. When the doctor came to see me at 9 o'clock all he said was, 'You gave us quite a turn this morning didn't you?' and I just smiled. From that moment I had lost my fear of death and I knew that all would be well, although it was to be another three months before I was discharged from the hospital."

After that, Karin had out-of-body experiences periodically while sleeping during which she "woke" to find herself in another part of the house before drifting back into her body. And then there were the strange incidents which followed her mother-in-law's death.

"Her name was Mary and she had been living with us for some time. I was acting as her nurse because, although she was lucid in her mind, physically she was very frail. One day she said to me that if it was at all possible she would come back after her death so that I would have proof of the survival of the soul. I didn't take it seriously at the time, but two months after her passing she did come back.

"One day, all the clocks in the house starting behaving strangely. They all showed a different time. One suddenly developed an erratic tick, another stopped altogether and a travelling alarm clock rolled off the bookshelf on to the floor to crash at my feet just as I was telling my daughter about how oddly they were all behaving. All she said was, 'spooky' and went out of the house.

"Another day I was alone in the house when the receiver jumped off the phone on the wall and started swinging from side to side. Then the electric blanket switched itself on and the toaster was pushed down, but no one had put any bread in the slots. I complained to my husband that I was feeling cold and getting goose pimples, but he just told me to see a doctor or forget it. But by then I knew I wasn't ill. It was Mary trying to tell me that she was with me.

"The final proof came when I went to a spiritualist meeting and was told by a medium, who I'd never met before, that my husband's mother was trying to communicate, that her name was Mary and that she had died of cancer, which was true. She just wanted to say thank you for all the time I had looked after her, that I had been good to her and that she would now look after me. She actually used to say that I had been good to her so that rang true as well. Then the medium said that Mary sent her love to my husband, my son and his girlfriend and she named them all which left me with my mouth wide open. The only thing I couldn't understand was that she said: 'I'm with Emma now' because I didn't know of an Emma in the family. Afterwards I learnt that Emma was Mary's sister who had died 11 years earlier. Mary had never mentioned Emma because she came from a very large family and I didn't ask too much about her past. Since then I have smelt Mary's talcum powder on many occasions and I knew then that she was watching over me."

Those who have little knowledge or experience of the spiritual realms often tend to dismiss all paranormal phenomena as a product of the unconscious mind because they fear the possibility of contact with an unspecified malevolent force. But practising mediums rarely have such qualms. Karin says:

"I personally don't believe in the Devil, but I do believe in evil as a force created by human energies. So I don't relate to evil as a reality. I subscribe to the universal law which states that like attracts like, which means that we create our own experiences through our thoughts and actions.

"I have, however, had experiences with people who have become disturbed after playing with Ouija boards where they have attracted earthbound spirits, but these are the restless spirits of human beings and not evil entities. You have to deal with them in the same way that you would deal with a violent drunk or drug addict who can't be reasoned with.

"I had one case where a 17-year-old girl came to me in great distress because the Ouija board had told her that she wouldn't live to see her 18th birthday. She really believed that she had been singled out for death because the first few messages that came through revealed details that none of the other people in the group at the seance could have known. I was able to reassure her that if she stopped giving it power by feeding it with her fear and instead visualised herself clothed in light and the love of the angels she would dispel the negative energy that she had attracted to herself. I told her that at midnight that night I would link in to her and send healing to calm and reassure her. First thing the next morning she phoned to tell me that at midnight she had felt an almost physical burden lift from her shoulders and a lightness envelop her like an angel's wings. She knew intuitively from that moment on that no harm would come to her. But she told me that that morning her mother had gone out into the garden to feed their pet rabbit which had been perfectly healthy the day before and she found that it was dead. Evidently whatever form this negative energy had taken it had to 'ground' itself somehow."

A MODERN MIRACLE?

MORE RECENTLY KARIN and I were both witness to a
miraculous cure that was given to a mutual friend of ours,
whom I shall call John for the purpose of this story. John
was a fit, elderly man who had been training as a spiritual
healer at the Star of the East centre. He was looking forward to completing the two-year course when he was diagnosed as having cancer of the pancreas, an incurable form
of the disease. The doctors admitted that there was nothing
they could do for him and they sent him home to die.

John later confided to me that his initial reaction to
being told the news was a feeling of elation, not because
he would eventually be free of pain, but because he was
overwhelmed by a sense that his life was playing out the
way it had been planned and that he would soon be going
"home." He didn't tell anybody about this at the time,
being more concerned with the feelings of his family who
were in a state of shock.

Karin and other local healers then began a course of
regular spiritual healing which involved the laying-on of
hands and channelling the universal life-force to the
affected area in order to kill the cancerous cells and stimulate the patient's own immune system. They also gave
him some vibhuti, or sacred ash, to place on the tip of his
tongue and on the "third eye" in the centre of his forehead
as a form of blessing, just as a Christian priest might make
the sign of the cross on a worshipper's forehead with holy
water. Vibhuti is said to be created by the Indian avatar Sai
Baba and is therefore believed to have miraculous properties (see page 134).

At this time, John was not a follower of Baba and knew
nothing about him. He had seen pictures of the holy man

at the Star of the East hall, but showed no interest in knowing more. He later told me that during one particularly uncomfortable night he saw Sai Baba appear at the end of his bed as solid and life-like as if he had been there in the flesh. John was overwhelmed by a feeling of compassion and selfless love emanating from the diminutive figure who simply smiled broadly and wagged his finger in a kindly mocking way. In a clear voice which seemed to come from within John's own head he heard Baba say: "You naughty man!" John told me that it was as if Baba was gently chiding him for giving in too readily and not trusting in his own innate healing powers.

PSYCHIC SURGERY

IT WAS AFTER this that John decided to put his faith in the hands of one of Britain's best known psychic surgeons, Stephen Turoff, who believes that his work is blessed by Baba. Turoff is one of many such healers who perform painless operations without anaesthetic in makeshift surgeries from South America to the suburbs of South London. Many, like Stephen, are untrained but are directed by their spirit guides, some of whom had been doctors in a previous life. Psychic surgery effects cures by working on the etheric body where the source of all "dis-ease" is believed to originate, rather than on the flesh where only the symptoms manifest. No anaesthetic is needed because the surgeon manipulates matter by raising its level of vibration so that he can plunge his hands inside the body without having to make an incision. Stephen's patients feel only the pressure of his fingers and the kneading of the flesh. For the duration of the operation he sinks into a light

trance during which he is taken over by his spirit guide, a
Viennese surgeon by the name of Dr. Kahn whose identity
and history have been verified by independent sources.

A friend or relative of the patient is allowed to witness
or even film the operation which is sometimes accompanied by a sloshing sound as Stephen's hands disappear
inside the body and occasionally by a plop or two as the
diseased tissue is dropped into a bucket! The gore, however, is invisible to physical sight and the diseased matter
instantly dematerialises. Stephen says that some patients
need to see blood before they can believe that he has really
done something to them, but so many were put off by it
that he asked spirit to leave it in its higher vibrational state
until it was removed from the body.

It sounds incredible, but innumerable patients have tes-
tified to the effectiveness of his treatments and scientific
studies have also verified the impressive results. A thorough five-year study by an American doctor, Linda Chard,
concluded:

> "We know that Stephen is not masquerading. I have seen
> [Dr. Kahn], dead to the earth plane, perform operations
> [through Stephen] that defy normal scientific interpreta-
> tion. My understanding of what Dr. Kahn does when
> dematerialising diseased tissue is that by altering the
> sub-atomic energy within the cellular structure of the
> tissue he is able to disperse it into recyclable matter."

I myself submitted to psychic surgery for a minor ailment
in January 1999 for the purpose of this book and although
I was not cured I certainly felt cleansed, almost purified,
after the experience. The closest I can come to describing
the sensation is to liken it to having the essence of one's

being shaken and then left to settle. There was nothing in Stephen's demeanour that convinced me that he was possessed by Dr. Kahn, but I had been affected by the energy that he transmitted to me and I was left with a thin three-inch scar which I made sure was seen by a number of witnesses before it vanished the following day.

Other patients in my party during that trip had mixed results. One man expressed disappointment that he had only been given slight relief from a painful leg complaint (although it continued to improve over the following weeks), but another bounded out of the treatment room overjoyed that a chronic backache that he had endured for 20 years had been cured in less than five minutes.

Karin admits that she was initially very sceptical about the many claims made for Stephen's miraculous cures and decided to test "Dr. Kahn." On her first visit to the Chelmsford clinic she took with her a recent letter from her mother which was written in German in which her mother described a visit she had made to her doctor. Karin knew that Stephen, a cockney with little formal education, could not speak any other language, but if he was genuine then "Dr. Kahn" certainly could. When she was called into the treatment room she produced the letter without giving any details and was surprised to hear "Dr. Kahn" read it under his breath in a heavy Austrian accent and conclude: "Yes, that is the correct diagnosis."

Of course, under the circumstances, Stephen could have assumed it concerned a medical matter. He said nothing specific about the illness. He has also travelled widely holding surgeries in many countries around the world and could easily have picked up a smattering of German in the process. However, subsequent events convinced Karin of Stephen's sincerity and his talents.

The doctors had given our friend John just six weeks to live, and offered him a choice of two types of treatment. He could have a course of chemotherapy or submit to surgery. Because no one had ever survived pancreatic cancer the surgeons only performed two such operations a year. John chose surgery because he thought that Dr. Kahn would assist on the psychic level and he was determined to walk back into the Star of the East hall under his own steam and complete his healing course. Initially he felt too ill and weak to make the journey to Stephen's clinic, but with each treatment he became progressively stronger and his spirits rose. By the fourth and final visit eight weeks later he amazed doctors by being the first person to survive pancreatic surgery and to reveal not a trace of cancerous cells thereafter. In fact, the medical team kept visiting him at home for weeks afterwards to ask how he had done it. Shortly after surgery he returned to the hall as he had promised himself, completed the course and began healing others.

The last time I saw him he was cheerful and looking extremely healthy and could boast of taking long walks again. But six months later the cancer returned, this time to the liver, and he died soon after. Karin feels that he had been given the help he needed, but that his time was up.

It is difficult to understand why someone suffering a terminal illness will be cured only to have it return at a later date, but in spiritualist circles there is a clear explanation for this. "We cannot go against what might be called God's will or indeed the will of our own higher self," says Karin.

"We have an allotted time, agreed upon with the higher self, in which to learn and experience whatever we need to in order to develop spiritually. In cases of recurring illness it could be said that not only the sufferer, but their whole family, learns from the experience. It has brought them to a better understanding which remains after their grief has gone. We have to accept that no matter how much we love somebody and wish them to remain with us, if it is their time to move on then they will go. It is my understanding that their suffering is more for the awakening of those that they leave behind. In a sense they sacrifice what is left of their time to awaken those around them and possibly also to clear a burden of karma that would otherwise take a lifetime or more to clear. Of course, if you are insensitive enough to tell someone that their loved one has chosen to suffer in this way they will think you're mad. They can't understand that it is the body which suffers temporally, not the immortal spirit which is using the body as a vehicle for spiritual evolution."

MY EXPERIENCES AS A HEALER

I BEGAN TENTATIVELY testing my own psychic talents in my early 30s after joining a meditation group which specialised in spiritual healing. It had seemed to me the ideal way to probe the unknown as I would be opening myself up for a positive purpose and always with the support of experienced healers.

The first time I practised healing on a volunteer, the woman remarked that the heat from my hands was as intense as a three-bar electric fire, but that it was a comforting heat and it "cured" the pain she was then suffering

from in her shoulders. The pain never returned. All I had
done was to enter a meditative state in which I was aware
of my surroundings but was at the same time detached
from the physical world. Then I silently invited the universal creative force to use me as a channel for the healing
energy, as I had been instructed to do, and I laid my hands
on the patient's shoulders so that I could direct whatever
came through me to the area of the body where it was
needed. When giving healing I felt no more than a tingling
sensation in my hands or the warmth that I was transmit-
ting.

Although the patients that I treated in this and subsequent healing groups experienced various degrees of heat
and a trance-like serenity, I was surprised by the subtlety
of the sensations that I felt. However, when I had forgotten
to prepare myself by visualising fibrous roots of etheric
energy anchoring me to the earth, I would become unbal-
anced by the surge of inflowing energy and rock back-
wards and forwards during the treatment like a sapling in
a storm!

It was understood by the healers that we were not the
source of this energy, but simply the channels, and that our
purpose was to be open to this divine force. If we tried to
will it to work for us, or force it through our bodies we
would only succeed in draining ourselves of vital energy.
The healers that I worked with all seem to have had similar experiences, but to have developed differing degrees of
sensitivity to their patients' needs.

Some spoke to me of being able to identify the areas of
the body which are in need of healing by feeling for "cold
spots" to which they then apply the heat from their hands.
It is as if the circulation of vital energy in the patient's
etheric body can become blocked, starving the chakras, or

centres of spiritual energy, of power, just as poor circulation of blood can starve the vital organs of oxygen in its physical counterpart. Others described images or colours that they saw in their mind's eye as they worked with a patient. The colours would be interpreted as corresponding to a specific chakra which the healer would attempt to stimulate by placing their hands on or over that spot and envisaging the universal life-force revitalising that energy centre in the etheric body.

Later I learnt to call upon my spirit guides and those of the patient to assist me with the healing and although I never saw these discarnate beings myself, others did and described them in detail. They usually appeared in the form of a Chinese person or a Native American Indian, presumably because natural medicine was a core element of these cultures and many would have chosen to continue their work on the inner planes after their own death.

But even before I had been told about the guides I felt their presence. During one of the first healing sessions that I did I felt a pair of hands under my own with a distinct but elastic form. It was similar to feeling the surface of a balloon. Under any other circumstances I imagine that I would have been unsettled by such an experience, but while healing it seemed entirely natural. It was only afterwards that I was surprised how calmly I had accepted the presence of spirits.

ON THE RECEIVING END

WHENEVER I RECEIVED healing myself, either for the purposes of learning what it was like to be on the receiving end or for a "top-up" whenever I was tired, I felt an intense heat from the healer's hands and I enjoyed a sense of serenity which permeated the very essence of my being. It always left me calm, cleansed and in a buoyant mood.

I no longer need convincing of the efficacy or the reality of spiritual healing; I have experienced its benefits for myself. It was only the degree of healing that varied with the individual who treated me.

Such a subtle exchange of energy does not prove in itself that we are capable of effecting real and lasting change to the physical body by repairing damaged tissue or treating cancerous cells for example. However, during the course of my time as a healer I was given what I believe to be conclusive proof of its potential for such miraculous cures on two occasions. On the first I was the subject seeking a cure, while the second was the story of John on page 180.

In my own case I had been suffering from a persistent pain in my lower back which had been diagnosed and treated repeatedly with some success by a qualified osteopath, but I was still finding it impossible to sit or stand in comfort for more than a few minutes. In 1997 I attended a meditation group and was singled out for "special treatment" by the man who was taking the session that evening. I had not mentioned my problem to anyone in the group, nor had I exhibited any obvious signs of discomfort that anyone would have noticed, although by the end of the evening I was in some pain. We were about to break the circle when the leader announced that his spirit guides had informed him that someone was in urgent need of healing. He asked everyone to remain in their seats and assist in the treatment by returning to a meditative state and holding their palms towards the centre of the circle to direct the healing energy. All of this might strike the sceptic as theatrical hokum, but what followed convinced me of the power of spiritual healing once and for all.

I was asked to stand in the centre of the circle and relax. The teacher held me lightly under the chin with one hand and supported the small of my back with the other. In a moment I lost all sense of my physical body and remained suspended in a state of weightlessness for some minutes. I felt no other sensation, nor was I aware of the presence of any discarnate beings working on me or any physical manipulation of the muscles. But when I regained my physical senses the pain had gone and it has never returned.

THE AURA

THE HEALING EXPERIENCE encouraged me to experiment in other areas. I had always been eager to see the aura, that radiance of etheric energy which is said to surround all living things as a visible expression of the life-force, but I hadn't been able to. It was only when I had been practising healing for two years that I finally saw it. I had been told by one of the healers that the "trick" was to look at your hand against a plain white background and soften your focus so that you looked beyond the hand to the surface behind it. After some practice I could see the pastel blue border very clearly tracing the outline of my hand and between my fingers. Later it appeared spontaneously surrounding people that I evidently felt an empathy with. I have not yet been able to see beyond this initial layer to the many colours that sensitives, or psychics, believe reveal the state of a person's health and mind, but

I am given to understand that this will occur as my awareness increases over the years.

MYSTERIES OF THE TAROT

ONE OF THE individuals with whom I felt an immediate affinity was a woman who taught me the mysteries of the Tarot cards and with whom I was later to organise a series of angel workshops. I had always associated the Tarot with occultism and was wary of "dabbling in the occult" which I have seen as distinct from the spiritual path. The latter I understood requires a person to follow a tradition in which they serve the greater good rather than their own self-interest, but this is a belief that I have since rejected. To serve the greater good we first have to know ourselves.

Although I was taught the traditional interpretation of the cards and shown how they could be used for divination I came to the conclusion that the cards themselves do not foretell the future, instead they serve to stimulate and focus our own predictive powers through their universal symbols. Our innate ability to anticipate future events using such means is supernatural only in the sense that it involves a heightened awareness of the subtle influences at work in our lives. There is no supernatural agency involved in selecting the cards. Their selection is as random as one would expect when dealing from a deck of regular playing cards. Their value is in the symbols which are relevant at any given moment to whomever chooses to consult them.

Their somewhat sinister reputation comes from their uncanny accuracy in helping the reader to predict future possibilities, and the presence of the ominous-looking quartet "Death," "The Hanged Man," "The Tower" and "The Devil." These cards are now more likely to be seen as signifying psychological states, qualities and failings, with Death signifying change, The Hanged Man representing indecision, The Tower symbolising false pride and The Devil suggesting the tendency to enslave ourselves through addiction, fear, greed or an over-eagerness to impress others.

PSYCHIC READINGS

I HAVE HAD a number of psychic readings over the years which have given me accurate information about future opportunities which came to pass as described. When I was a teenager, a close family member had a momentary vision in which she saw me and a number of friends travelling in a white car through the mountains of a Mediterranean country. She also sensed that we were extremely happy at that moment. Several years later I toured Greece as part of a rock band. We travelled in a white car (which was itself unusual as we normally travelled in a van) and one afternoon we passed scenery strikingly similar to that which she had described. We were all in an elated mood having played a wonderful concert the night before.

Of course I did not share this vision and cannot prove that the image and the reality were the same, but I have no reason to doubt that this was a genuine example of future sight. I believe it was the emotional charge which created this link and that such insights are possible because we are in essence pure consciousness and that when we raise our consciousness beyond physical perception we transcend both time and space.

PSYCHIC INSIGHT

PSYCHIC INSIGHT COMES in many forms. Some intuitives read the aura of their clients, others get an impression by handling something which belongs to the sitter, while others can even make a link through the phone lines. A few years ago I would have doubted that such an impersonal approach could be possible, but I have received valuable guidance from a celebrated psychic with whom I talked on the phone and I have witnessed several remarkable demonstrations of this kind as psychics revealed personal details about complete strangers which were subsequently confirmed. I must make a distinction here between the genuine intuitives who give lengthy and corroborative evidence of their gifts and the educated guesswork practised by employees of the commercial "psychic" telephone lines which are of little value to anyone.

PAST-LIFE REGRESSION

ONE OF THE most fascinating forms of psychic reading is that which can reveal details of our past lives. Unfortunately many people seek a past-life reading in the hope of discovering that they were a celebrated historical figure and are invariably disappointed.

It is my belief that one should only seek knowledge of a past life in order to illuminate the present. I have been cured of a life-long phobia simply by having the source of this fear revealed to me during a reading. I have also discovered that there is a logical pattern to my various incarnations all of which have contributed to creating my current personality. I have been led to understand that in each life we also have the opportunity to "clear" certain karmic debts arising from our past actions or to revise our attitudes to certain things. Being preoccupied with the routine concerns of our lives we are not always conscious of these underlying impulses, and such details can be revealed by a reading. These sessions can take the form of a face-to-face reading in which the intuitive tunes in to the sitter, reading the impressions in their aura, listening to details supplied by their spirit guides, or scanning the Akashic Records which hold an impression of our past actions. In such circumstances the sitter takes the information on trust and has to decide for themself what is significant and true for them.

The other form of past-life reading involves a form of hypnotic regression in which the client is put into a state of deep relaxation and is encouraged to explore the images which come spontaneously to mind. The therapist should not make any suggestions or seek to influence what is seen. I have experienced regression on one occasion and was impressed by the vivid detail of the imagery which came to mind which was quite distinct from the vague, fleeting images of the imagination. These past-life impressions arose spontaneously and could not be altered at will. I could explore an entire house at my leisure during which time the imagery remained stable. I could then return to a particular room and find it just the way I had left it, whereas imaginary scenes alter with the fluidity of a dream. Once I had probed the past in this way, memories and scenes of past lives began to appear spontaneously during my regular meditations, each having the same quality of vivid detail. But the most convincing aspect was the people who appeared fully formed and absorbed in their own affairs. They were "real" personalities from the past that I could not have imagined at will. The value of such experiences as I see it is to give us a fuller understanding of who we are and why we hold the attitudes that we do.

18

DREAMS—BEYOND THE REALM OF SLEEP

EACH OF US spends an average of 25 years of our lives in the sleeping state and yet we are still without a satisfactory explanation as to why sleep is necessary, or what the significance of our dreams may be. Many people deny that they dream at all. However, scientific research has identified the brainwave patterns characteristic of dream activity which prove that we all dream, even if we cannot recall doing so. But perhaps the most inexplicable aspect of the phenomenon is the fact that the majority of people express little or no curiosity concerning the nature of dreams and dismiss their own nocturnal wanderings as mere fantasy despite considerable anecdotal evidence that dreams are the gateway to a greater reality.

The common belief is that sleep is vital for physical and mental health, that it is a resting period for the body and the brain during which consciousness appears to be suspended. But clinical research has proven that whilst specific muscles need periodic rest, neither the brain nor the body are inactive during sleep. Even the most sedate sleeper alters their position occasionally throughout the night to keep the blood circulating through the limbs, muscles and joints. Moreover, most of the vital organs do not need cyclic periods of rest, and nor does the brain, which in certain phases of sleep often exhibits sustained bursts of activity which can exceed those recorded during the waking state.

Yet researchers have discovered that depriving people of sleep for more than a few days can have serious and even permanent consequences for their emotional and physical well-being. The initial symptoms of sleep deprivation are irritability, depression, paranoia and hallucinations (which become increasingly disturbing). But these temporary aberrations can be cured by a lengthy sleep which leaves the subject with no lasting ill-effects. Other experiments have shown that dreaming is equally as essential. Subjects who were repeatedly woken as they entered the dreaming phase eventually exhibited similar psychological disturbances to those characteristic of sleep deprivation, as the cumulative effect of dream deprivation took hold. When they were eventually allowed to sleep through the full cycle they made up for the loss of dream time with measurable extended phases of dream sleep.

THE STAGES OF SLEEP

THERE ARE FIVE distinct stages of sleep which were identified by American scientist Nathaniel Kleitman and his colleagues in the 1950s after studying the brainwaves and eye movements of scores of subjects. Four of these stages are characterised by thoughts rather than dreams, which might explain why we often wake with an impression of only the most trivial and absurd dreams. These would be the random jumble of subconscious thoughts experienced prior to awakening as we ascend from the depths of the unconscious to the waking state.

Only when we awake suddenly from deep sleep would we retain the detailed impressions and sense of other levels of reality, of the spiritual dimensions, which we can access involuntarily during sleep. These experiences, which can include astral projection, prophetic dreams and the so-called "great dreams," identified by Carl Jung, of revelationary insight are characteristic of the fifth stage known as rapid eye movement or REM sleep when our most vivid dreams occur.

This phase is also known as "the paradoxical phase" because while the body lies limp and oblivious to external stimuli our brainwaves indicate alertness often accompanied by a measurable secretion of adrenaline as if we are alerting the body for imminent action. The eyes of the dreamer flit rapidly from side to side during this phase, but scientific opinion is divided as to its significance. Some maintain that this is a mere reflex, while others suggest that the eyes are scanning images of an imaginary movie behind the eyelids and they cite occasions when these movements appear to correspond with events in the dream.

THE PSYCHOLOGY OF SLEEP

ORTHODOX SCIENCE DEFINES dreaming as an electro-biological processing function of the brain in which our memories and impressions are sifted in an apparently random and purposeless fashion. As such, it attaches no significance to the images of the dreamscape, but accepts that the various brainwave patterns associated with the stages of sleep appear to indicate differing levels of consciousness.

In contrast, psychoanalysts attribute great significance to the symbolism of our dreams, which they consider to be the language of the unconscious, although they invariably disagree as to its meaning. Followers of Sigmund Freud, the father of modern psychoanalysis, refer to dreams as "the royal road to the unconscious" and see their symbolism as often expressing the dreamer's suppressed wishes and sexual fantasies.

Freud's former pupil Carl Jung, however, interpreted the symbols as archetypal images which signify common instincts and experiences shared by all humanity. He visualised these as existing at a primal level of the psyche which he called the Collective Unconscious to which we have access in moments of contemplation and in the deepest stages of sleep. Ironically the principal concepts of Jung's philosophy were revealed to him in a dream in which he found himself in a house whose various levels corresponded to the levels of the psyche and of awareness. With its refined decor and lived-in atmosphere the salon could be seen as being symbolic of waking consciousness while the basement had the appearance of a cave. Here Jung discovered relics of a prehistoric culture which he interpreted as symbolising his own primitive nature.

Modern psychologists, counsellors and therapists agree that dreams can provide a valuable source of material for understanding the motivations behind our behaviour and attitudes. However, they tend to interpret the symbols in terms of the individual personality and background of their patient rather than as a manifestation of the Collective Unconscious.

Californian psychologist and dream-work specialist Strephon Kaplan-Williams believes that dream imagery reflects our inner state and that we should see it as crucial to the process of integrating all aspects of our personality. Kaplan-Williams considers dreams to be the key to discovering our true self which is represented by our dream ego, the image of ourself which we project into our dreams. But instead of analysing our dreams he urges us to actualise them, to make them real by aiming to resolve the problems with which they present us in the waking world.

A similar view is shared by Gestalt therapists. Gestalt therapy was devised in the U.S. during the 1960s and encouraged patients to focus on the present and to express their true feelings. Gestalt therapists ask their patients to act out their significant dreams, taking each role in turn in the belief that each character is a facet of the dreamer's own personality. In this way patients are encouraged to reclaim aspects of their personality that they might have "disowned" or denied, and in so doing they become themselves rather than who they believe they ought to be.

THE SLEEPING SOLUTION

DESPITE THE EFFORTS of psychologists to explore the unconscious, the scientific establishment continues to dismiss all dreams as part of a purely physiological process— mere fantasies—even though dreams have repeatedly proved to be the inspiration for numerous inventions and have offered the solution to many a scientific conundrum.

A dream helped the chemist Friedrich Von Kekule (1829–1896), for example, to identify the molecular structure of benzene. In the dream, Kekule saw snake-like chains of atoms swallowing their tails which gave him the solution—the molecular structure of benzene was a closed carbon ring. The physicist Niels Bohr (1885–1962) discovered the structure of the atom in a similar dream, while the Nobel Prize–winning chemist Albert Szent-Gyorgyi (1893–1986) regularly trusted his unconscious mind to provide a solution during sleep after he had exhausted the intellectual approach.

Giving our problems over to a higher power has long been a method advocated by mystics and the religiously inclined, but it appears that we all have the capacity to tap this source of knowledge through our dreams regardless of our religious beliefs.

In 1983 Morton Schatzman, an American psychiatrist, set the readers of a national magazine a mathematical conundrum to which they were to seek the solution in their dreams. The problem was how to construct four equilateral triangles from six line segments of equal length when the sides of the triangle were the same length as the segments. They were to ponder the problem just before drifting off to sleep and write down details of any dream which seemed relevant. Of the dozens of correct solutions which Schatzman received one was from a schoolgirl who dreamt that she was running her fingers along a panel of railings when six rods jumped out of their sockets to form a wigwam, the only three-dimensional form to contain four equilateral triangles. In a subsequent scene of the same dream she found herself sitting an exam and pondering over the same problem. As she did so, her chemistry teacher appeared and gave her the second part of the answer which was 109 degrees 28 minutes. This figure corresponds to what is known as the bond angle, a complex geometrical form composed of four equilateral triangles found in molecular chemistry. Either this obscure detail had been stored in the depths of her unconscious mind or there is, as mystics maintain, a higher all-knowing aspect of our personality which has the answers.

PROPHETIC DREAMS

IN THE ANCIENT world meaningful dreams were considered the exclusive preserve of prophets and kings. One of the earliest prophetic dreams to be recorded was that which led Pharaoh Thutmose IV to discover the Sphinx in 1,450 BCE. The monument had been buried under the sand for centuries until Thutmose dreamt that he was visited by the god Hormakhu and ordered to clear the sand from the site.

But in modern times there are many ordinary people who claim to have experienced precognitive dreams and to have travelled beyond the realm of sleep to glimpse a greater reality.

In 1913 Carl Jung dreamt of a river of blood and bloated corpses which swept through Europe. The vision was repeated a fortnight later accompanied by a voice which assured him that what he was witnessing was not a nightmare but a coming reality. Other disturbing dreams followed featuring the mythical hero Siegfried (a German Prince who slew the dragon that guarded the treasure of the Nibelung and, in turn, was murdered by a jealous rival) and archetypal symbols of death and rebirth, the significance of which became clear to Jung a year later with the outbreak of World War I. Jung had experienced prophetic dreams since childhood and was convinced that the unconscious mind was the source of all paranormal phenomena, intuitive insights and inspiration.

Celebrated psychic Edgar Cayce (1877–1945) was known as the "sleeping prophet" due to his habit of sinking into a sleep-like trance from which he emerged with miracle cures and uncannily accurate predictions. On one occasion it is believed that he prescribed a cure for a disease and identified the pharmaceutical company which made the drug just hours before it was named and approved for manufacture! His financial forecasts were equally remarkable, although he refused to profit by his predictions. In early March 1929, at a time when the stock market was enjoying an unprecedented boom, he warned an investor of a disastrous drop in share prices which would continue for some time. He repeated his warning the following month and was proved correct six months later when the Wall Street Crash wiped millions off the value of shares and brought about the Great Depression.

Cayce attributed his gift to his ability to access to what he called the Universal Consciousness, a stream of collective knowledge similar to Jung's Collective Unconscious, which Cayce envisaged as being an etheric energy field on the astral plane.

The extent of precognitive experiences among ordinary people suggests that it is not an extraordinary gift but a natural faculty that we all share. It is particularly common among people with a strong emotional, and therefore psychic, bond with members of their family. There are many recorded incidents in the archives of various institutes for psychical research detailing the dreams of mothers who have "seen" their soldier sons in mortal danger, or actually being killed in the manner in which they did meet their death. Sometimes these dreams have occurred repeatedly during the boy's childhood accompanied by a suffocating sense of foreboding, so that the mother is convinced that it was more than a nightmare.

Other parents have dreamt of their child's death at what they later learnt was the fatal moment, again with the conviction that it was not merely a dream. But in one instance the recurrent nightmares caused a German mother to wake one night in February 1945 and pray for her son's safe return. She subsequently learnt that that night her son had been among a group of prisoners taken by the Russians. They were being systematically executed when a Russian officer intervened and spared the survivors. Her son had been the next man in line.

Not all precognitive dreams are concerned with death. There is the famous case of Lord Kilbraken, the Irish peer, who in 1946 repeatedly dreamt of the names of winning racehorses and won a considerable sum as a result. Lord Kilbraken's claims to precognitive powers were confirmed by his family and friends who all profited from his predictions, although their winning streak did not last. Initially Kilbraken had trusted his intuition that the dreams were significant and he acted upon them, thereby strengthening the link with the unconscious, but later he presumably became blasé and his psychic perception or dream recall declined.

It appears that we need to make an effort of will to cultivate this sensitivity if the phenomenon is to be repeated.

GLIMPSES OF A GREATER REALITY

THE POSSIBILITY THAT sleep involves suspension of the waking mind and can lead to a temporary separation of the spirit from the body was first proposed by the Dutch physicist Frederick Van Eeden in 1904. Van Eeden's own out-of-body experiences led him to the discovery of what is commonly called "lucid dreaming" in which the dreamer becomes aware that they are dreaming and then takes control of the dream. This usually occurs when we find ourselves in a situation that is too bizarre to believe, such as climbing a mountain in our underwear, and we literally wake up to the realisation that what seemed so real was a fantasy.

This is possible because, at that point, consciousness is focused or centred in what Van Eeden called the "dream body" which has also been known as the astral, etheric or spirit body. The vital functions of the physical body continue to operate, but in a state similar to that of a plane switched to autopilot. Once fully conscious in the dream body, which is our "natural" state, we are then able to explore the non-physical realms, specifically the astral plane whose finer elastic-like matter takes form according to our thoughts.

Lucid dreams invariably involve flying because this is the sensation we experience once the dream body is floating free of the physical. Dreams of falling usually precede waking up because this is the feeling of returning to the physical. We all experience lucid dreaming and astral travel, perhaps for short periods every night or maybe only when we are deeply relaxed, but few can recall the experience because it is usually followed by more dreams at the superficial levels of sleep which obscure its significance.

Moreover, it is the nature of the ego to deny the existence of anything which does not conform to the physical world in which it has its existence.

Glimpses of this greater reality, or "great dreams," do not involve astral projection but rather a heightening of awareness to a spiritual level beyond the astral plane. They can be experienced by anyone, although they tend to be visited upon those who have endured a crisis which has left them questioning the purpose of existence. Such visions often reveal the underlying unity of existence in symbolic form which the individual is later at a loss to describe, for language is incapable of describing that which is beyond human understanding. But they always leave a profound and lasting impression on the dreamer whose perception of life is positively transformed.

The British playwright J. B. Priestley, who was obsessively interested in the paradoxical nature of time, once dreamt of a vast armada of birds who aged and died as he watched them passing across the sky. He felt an overwhelming sense of waste and that all suffering was in vain. But then as he watched the birds, they sped up as if they were mere images in a movie seen in accelerated motion and he saw a white flame flickering through the blur of feathers. In that moment he was struck by the realisation that the flame was the life-force itself and that the purpose of all life was to be a vehicle for this divine spark. Individual suffering was of little consequence other than to serve the purpose of evolution, or the creative force.

19

SEEING DOUBLE

THE PHENOMENON OF "seeing double" (witnessing a vision or apparition of a person who is still alive) can be divided into five categories: doppelgangers, phantasms, phantom thought-forms, crisis apparitions and phantom forerunners.

DOPPELGANGERS

IT IS GENERALLY accepted that each of us has a physical double somewhere in the world, someone who is so strikingly similar in appearance that at first sight our family and friends could mistake them for us. Most us have mistaken strangers that we have glimpsed at a distance for people we know, or have been struck by the uncanny resemblance of celebrity look-alikes who exploit their similarity to the stars. Superficial physical similarities such as these, however, do not explain the strange phenomenon known as the

doppelganger (from the German "doublewalker") in which
witnesses claim to have seen solid apparitions of living
persons who were elsewhere at the time and, more rarely,
cases where an individual has been shocked to see their
own "ghost"!

The earliest recorded incident of this kind was
described by the Greek philosopher Aristotle in the 4th
century BCE, who wrote of a man who was literally
haunted by his double to the extent that the victim was
afraid to venture outside his house.

But the belief that we each have an independent spirit
personality can be traced back to the earliest civilisations
and is common to many cultures, both ancient and modern.

The ancient Persians conceived of two creators, a good
and an evil god, who each invested humans with a good
and a bad spirit which are continually at war with each
other. The ancient Egyptians described man as having
three souls of increasingly refined matter of which the Ka
was known as the "double," while the Greeks used the
word *daemon*, simply meaning spirit, to describe a person's spirit double. This term has since been corrupted to
denote an exclusively evil entity. No fewer than 57
cultures in the modern world believe in some form of spirit
double which dwells within each human being and can be
perceived as a mirror image of the physical form.

It is thought that the pagan belief in a shadow self
became the basis of the early Christian concept of the
guardian angel and that scriptural references to St. Paul
ascending through the heavens "in the spirit" was a
reference to an out-of-body experience, or astral projection.

The Catholic Church acknowledges the existence of
this phenomenon, but states that it is an ability reserved

exclusively for individuals of great sanctity. Nevertheless, the superstitious tended to view the appearance of living phantoms as harbingers of death. This notion has persisted into more enlightened times.

Shortly before her death in 1603 Queen Elizabeth I was said to have been shaken to see herself lying on her deathbed looking "pallid, shrivelled and wan." Another case of the period was described by John Aubrey, the 17th-century English folklorist, who recorded the experience of Lady Diana Rich who had seen her own apparition strolling through her father's garden at Kensington a month before she died of smallpox. And the poet Percy Bysshe Shelley claimed to have seen his own ghost shortly before he drowned in a boating accident in 1822.

A more baffling encounter was that experienced by Goethe, the 19th-century German poet and dramatist, who was riding home from visiting a sweetheart in Alsace when he saw his doppelganger approaching dressed in a grey and gold suit. The apparition lasted just a few seconds and Goethe, not being a superstitious man, thought little more of it. However, eight years later, he was passing the same spot on his way to visit the same girl when he realised that he was wearing the grey and gold suit of the "vision." The day had no special significance for him, leaving him to conclude that he had experienced a random glimpse of his future self perceived "with the eyes of the spirit," although he was at a loss as to how such things could be possible.

On a separate occasion Goethe had another strange experience in which he saw a friend walking some distance ahead dressed in one of his own dressing gowns. When he arrived home he found the friend warming himself by the fire wrapped in the very same dressing gown. The other man had decided to pay Goethe a surprise visit and had been caught in a sudden shower. He knew that his host would not mind if he borrowed his dressing gown while his own clothes were drying and this thought must have manifested itself in some form of sympathetic vision to Goethe some distance away.

Artists, poets and writers seem to be more prone to such experiences, possibly because they develop their intuitive and imaginative faculties to a greater extent than ordinary mortals. It is thought that intuition is the voice of our spirit, or higher self, and that imagination is the filter through which we glimpse the greater reality beyond the physical world. Creative individuals are therefore constantly in the process of strengthening the link between the conscious and unconscious mind in their search for inspiration and tend to trust in the impressions that come through more so than do "rational" personalities.

At a crucial point in his career the French author Guy de Maupassant received inspiration in a more direct manner than even he could have imagined. One day in 1885, de Maupassant was suffering from writer's block when a figure entered his study and began to dictate the next segment of the story. The writer was too stunned to complain about the intrusion for the stranger was his very own double. After a few moments the apparition faded leaving de Maupassant to continue the tale in the manner indicated. *The Horla* became one of the author's most celebrated stories and centres on a man who is possessed of a twin evil spirit which torments him until he is driven insane—a fate shared by de Maupassant himself who died in an asylum in 1893.

PHANTOM THOUGHT-FORMS AND BILOCATION

SEVERAL CHRISTIAN SAINTS are said to have been able to project their spirit double to another location. Legend has it that St. Anthony of Padua appeared before two congregations simultaneously at churches in Limoges on Holy Thursday in the year 1226 after he had inadvertently made commitments to attend both services. There were also several reliable witnesses to the appearance of St. Alphonsus de'Liguori at the deathbed of Pope Clement XIV in 1774 at the same time as de'Liguori was in meditation at a monastery in Arezzo. News of the pontiff's death had not yet reached the monastery when de'Liguori emerged from his reverie with a detailed description of the scene and the people attending the dying pontiff, all of which was subsequently confirmed by witnesses to the event.

Politicians are not commonly considered sensitive nor imaginative, but there are two famous cases of politicians unconsciously projecting life-like images of themselves in full view of reliable witnesses.

In January 1865 Charles Good, a member of the Legislative Council of British Columbia, appeared with other members of the Council for a group photograph. It was only later that they learnt that Good had only been there in spirit, for at the time of the sitting he was lying in a coma at his home attended by a doctor and concerned relatives.

In 1905 Sir Frederick Carne Rasch, a member of the British Parliament, contracted influenza and was ordered to stay in bed by his physician. This did not, however, prevent him from appearing on the back benches of the House of Commons during a debate where he was seen by other MPs. One of the other members, Sir Gilbert Parker, later admitted to a newspaper reporter that he had been aston-

ished to see Sir Frederick in attendance as everyone had
been informed that he was ill, but he was even more dumb-
founded when he looked again a moment later and noticed
that Sir Frederick had disappeared. Sir Frederick was not
at all surprised to learn that he had been seen in the House
as he had been very anxious to attend the debate. He evidently accepted that he had willed himself to appear, but
on his return he quickly tired of being prodded by his colleagues who were keen to confirm that he was no mere
phantom!

Incidents of conscious thought projection are more
numerous than one might imagine but in the majority of
cases the individual is not aware that their "ghost" is on the
loose.

In 1845 a 32-year-old French schoolmistress, Emilie
Sagée, despaired of finding a new post because she had
been dismissed from no fewer than 17 schools in just 16
years. Emilie was a good teacher, but she had the
unsettling habit of appearing in two places at once, a phenomenon known as bilocation. Her double appeared whenever she was tired and her mind wandered—a clue perhaps
to the source of the shadowy other self. Moreover, witnesses noticed that the appearance of the ghostly double
had a noticeable effect on the teacher whose movements
slowed as if she had become an automaton and left her
drained of vital energy.

Fortunately Emilie found a new post at a finishing
school at Neuwelcke, in Latvia but her ghostly double followed her there too. Soon after her arrival Emilie and her
apparition were seen standing side by side, the two moving in perfect unison at the blackboard in front of the entire
class. But the "reflection" vanished as soon as the teacher
turned to see the source of the commotion that she had

caused. On another occasion, Emilie was adjusting the dress of a pupil, Antonie Von Wrangel, who fainted when she saw two Emilies in the mirror. The double was next seen standing behind the teacher at the communal dinner table, an appearance which was witnessed by several of the school's servants. The presence of Emilie's double put paid to the possibility that the previous reports had been schoolgirl pranks.

Not long after this the entire school was assembled for embroidery practice in a large room overlooking the garden. From there they could see Emilie tending the flowers. After a few moments the supervising teacher left the girls alone, but her vacant chair was immediately occupied by Emilie's ghost! One girl tentatively approached the apparition which remained mute and motionless as she touched it, later describing it as feeling like muslin. Then it vanished. All the while the other Emilie could be seen moving amongst the flowers in the garden. She later admitted that she had noticed the other teacher leaving the room and had wished that she could be there to supervise the girls.

After this incident parents began to remove their children from the school which prompted the governors to dispense with Emilie's services. She went to live with her sister-in-law and promptly faded from public view.

Such episodes are not as uncommon as we might imagine. There are so many authenticated cases of bilocation that they cannot be readily dismissed as mere illusions. It is likely that such apparitions may be thought-forms; projections of the human mind which lack a separate consciousness. The conscious and deliberate creation of thought-forms has long been a part of mystical training in many esoteric orders and continues to be so. In the Tibetan Buddhist tradition, for example, these thought-forms are known as Tulpa Creations and the ability to produce them is considered to be an essential mental discipline. We all produce thought-forms unconsciously when we daydream or visualise someone whom we have strong feelings for. The images in our mind's eye are projected on to the astral plane, but generally disperse like cigarette smoke unless we will them into being by brooding on them repeatedly and charging them with intense emotion. Accepting such phenomena as being natural extensions of our minds may go some way towards explaining the nature of the etheric body.

Bilocation may be an inexplicable phenomenon to Westerners, but in the East the conscious separation of the spirit from the body is not considered so extraordinary. In *Autobiography of a Yogi*, Parahansa Yogananda, who was largely responsible for introducing yoga to the West in the 1940s, relates an occasion when a visiting yogi informed him that he was to expect a friend that had not been invited. In due course the friend arrived and made no apologies for his surprise visit for he claimed to have met Yogananda's visitor in the street some distance away and been informed that he was expected. This meeting between the unexpected guest and the yogi had evidently occurred while Yogananda and the yogi were deep in conversation.

CRISIS APPARITIONS

IN THE MAJORITY of cases the separation of body and spirit is spontaneous and usually precipitated by a crisis which provides a shock to the psyche. A crisis apparition usually appears to someone whom the apparition wishes to communicate something to before he or she dies. Depending on their powers of projection at that particular moment and the urgency of their message they can appear as a faint, transparent phantom-like figure or materialise in another part of the world in a manner that fools their host into believing they are actually there in the physical. The most extraordinary example of the latter was related in one of the earliest accounts of astral projection to be published, Robert Dale Owen's *Footfalls on the Boundary of Another World* (1860). According to Owen, one day in 1828 Robert Bruce, the first mate on a cargo ship, reported seeing a stranger in the captain's cabin. Bruce had interrupted the figure who was writing something on a slate, but he didn't wait to question the man whom he took to be a stowaway. The dreadful look on the man's face was enough to send Bruce scurrying up to the deck to rouse the captain himself. But when the captain went below he found the cabin empty and a message, "steer to the nor'west," scrawled on the slate.

The captain naturally assumed that they had a stowaway aboard and ordered a thorough search of the ship, but no one was found. He then ordered Bruce and every other member of the crew to copy the same message on the reverse of the slate in the belief that someone was playing a practical joke. To his surprise none of the men's writing was comparable to that of the stranger. Being somewhat superstitious, and erring on the side of caution, he ordered a change of course to the north-west.

Three hours later the look-out spotted a ship pinned against an iceberg and only minutes from being crushed to matchwood. As the lifeboat was unloading the last shivering survivors Bruce came face to face with the "ghost" that he had seen in the captain's cabin earlier that day. The man's writing proved to be the very same as had been found on the slate, although he had no explanation why it should be so. All he knew was that he had earlier fallen asleep from exhaustion and had dreamt of being aboard a ship that was coming to the rescue. When he awoke he told the others of his dream and gave them a detailed description of the ship, a fact subsequently confirmed by the other survivors.

While mute, spectral-like doubles can be created at will, they are quite distinct from those who make a full materialisation in order to convey a crucial message. This suggests that the degree of materialisation may depend upon the level of emotion with which the thought-form is animated. The number of hauntings in which the ghosts appear unaware of living witnesses suggests that an intense emotional charge experienced at a crucial moment in time can leave an impression in the ether just like light on movie film. This emotional imprint can then re-emerge at a later date, giving rise to the ghostly apparition. Such a notion is impossible to prove at present, but the following case gives credence to this explanation.

In 1987, *Time Life* magazine published the account of a mother who entered her child's bedroom to see an image of herself stooping over the bed wearing a dress she had not worn for some time. The image, which appeared to be grieving, promptly vanished. The woman later recalled that she had worn that dress while laying out the body of one of her children who had died three months before.

PHANTOM FORERUNNERS

NORWAY APPEARS TO be particularly prone to a rare type of spirit double known as a *vardogr*, or "phantom forerunner," so much so that it has given rise to the saying, "Is that you, or your vardogr?" whenever someone is early for an appointment. However, these phantoms are usually auditory rather than visual. Wiers Jensen, a student at the University of Oslo at the turn of the century, is said to have had a vardogr who regularly alerted his landlady that he was on his way home by rattling the front door knob or making phantom footsteps around the boarding house. His commitments at the university meant that his movements were unpredictable, but as soon as his landlady heard his vardogr she knew to put his dinner on so that it was ready by the time he arrived in person! The same is said to have been true of Oslo University professor Thorstein Wereide who was a member of Norway's Society for Psychical Research in the 1950s. Professor Wereide believed that such phenomena were common throughout the world but that Norwegians were particularly sensitive to them because they were a rural people. "Nature," he explained, "seems to have made use of 'supernatural' means to compensate for this isolation."

THE SCIENTIFIC EXPLANATION

ATTEMPTS HAVE BEEN made at a rational explanation for these phenomena, but whilst they may account for individual sightings they fail to explain those which were described independently by several witnesses.

The clinical definition of a doppelganger describes the apparition as being a life-sized mirror image of a living person which is invariably of a ghostly transparency, often in monochrome or having "washed-out" colours. A doppelganger does not appear solid and convincingly life-like or act independently as Robert Bruce's stowaway is said to have done, but instead replicates the movements and expressions of its physical counterpart as if it was a reflection. More significantly, the clinical definition of a doppelganger hallucination, or "autoscopy," only allows for a partial apparition, never the full figure, which again does not conform to the experiences described. The experience itself is rare and tends to occur at dawn or late at night to people under stress or severely fatigued.

Although the phenomenon has been subjected to little serious study it is a clinically recognised condition which is classified as a visual hallucination. But it is not exclusively a visual phenomenon. Many subjects claimed that they could sense and hear their doubles which, according to Graham F. Reed, Chairman of the Department of Psychology at Glendon College, York University, Toronto, suggests that the experience may be linked to a manifestation of displaced memories.

Reed's theory is that it may be a hallucinatory effect of epilepsy and cerebral disorders. He has observed that the experience is more common among delirious patients, those with brain lesions in the parieto-occipital regions and as a side-effect of partial seizures in epileptics. But it can also occur for a few seconds in normal people as a feature of a migraine attack. In extreme cases the subject may even see himself in another room, an occurrence known as an extracampine hallucination. It may be significant that doppelgangers have been featured in the work of several famous authors who are believed to have suffered epilepsy or cerebral disorders, namely Dostoevsky, de Maupassant, Kafka, Steinbeck, Oscar Wilde and Edgar Allan Poe.

The possibility that phantoms of both the living and the dead might be externalisations of consciousness was given serious thought by the otherwise pragmatic Sigmund Freud. In 1919, Freud published a paper entitled *The Uncanny* in which he suggested that the idea of us all having an immortal soul originated in prehistory when our ancestors feared death to the extent that their conscious mind denied the reality of their own mortality. For Freud, such mystical concepts were an expression of self-love which both society and the individual should lose if they are to mature and progress. However, in private Freud is known to have been fascinated by the paranormal and to have advocated psychic research as a legitimate scientific enterprise. He was clearly in two minds himself when it came to belief in the supernatural for in 1905 he caught a glimpse of his own double and although he was convinced it was simply a case of a striking physical resemblance, Freud confided to his friends that it meant he was going to die. Instead, he lived for another 34 years, dying at the age of 83.

20

POLTERGEISTS

THE POLTERGEIST PHENOMENON has haunted para-psychologists for more than a century and yet they have been unable to offer a rational explanation for the extraordinary and often violent disturbances which are traditionally attributed to malevolent spirits.

Reports of poltergeist activity date back to the 1st century AD when Theoderic (?454–526 AD), King of the Ostrogoths—a group of Goths in the east of the region who established a Kingdom in Italy from 493 to 552 AD—is said to have been besieged by an invisible adversary who bombarded his palace with stones. Since then there have been innumerable reported incidents through the centuries, of which over 1,000 have been thoroughly documented and investigated in modern times.

In 1992, for example, a Portsmouth family called in a priest and several psychics to witness the unsettling sight of their furniture moving by itself and to hear a cacophony of strange noises and experience unpleasant odours which

had plagued them for several months. The experts agreed
that the focus of the disturbances was the family's 18-
month-old daughter Jasmin who appeared to have been
befriended by the earthbound spirit of a former tenant. He
was frequently heard to speak in a pronounced Northern
accent using the toddler as a medium which unsettled the
parents even more than the physical damage he caused. In
desperation the family threatened to withhold payment of
the rent until the local council agreed to repair the damage
caused by the poltergeist. Council officials are said still to
be investigating the authenticity of the claim.

PSYCHOKINESIS AND THE ROSENHEIM CASE

ALTHOUGH THE WORD "poltergeist" derives from the
German term for a noisy ghost, there is increasing evidence that in some cases the disturbances might be the
unconscious creation of the "victims" who are practising
an involuntary form of psychokinesis (PK) which enables
them to move objects using the power of the mind. In one
of the most famous incidents on record, known as the
Rosenheim case, the disturbances were traced to an 18-
year-old girl whose neurotic disposition appeared to have
triggered what amounted to a psychic temper tantrum.

In November 1967, Sigmund Adam, a solicitor with a
small practice in Rosenheim near Munich, called in the
local lighting company to investigate an increasing number of electrical faults in his office. The strip lights had
been failing on a regular basis and the meter had registered
inexplicable surges of current. In the course of their tests
the electricians discovered that their voltmeters registered
3 volts when connected to a 1.5-volt battery which was

simply not possible. Something was evidently affecting the supply. The lighting company installed a generator in order to bypass the powerlines and advised Adam to replace the strip lights with bulbs, but the power surges continued, shattering the bulbs in the process. A second generator failed to solve the problem, and then other anomalies began to occur. A massively inflated telephone bill showed that someone in the office was dialling the speaking clock continually for several hours every day although none of the staff had been using the phone. Moreover, it was being dialled up to six times a minute which was an impossibility as it took 17 seconds or more to make each call. Something was evidently bypassing the dialling mechanism and getting straight through to the relays. About this time more classic poltergeist activity manifested itself. On two occasions a heavy filing cabinet moved away from the wall, apparently by itself, and pictures revolved on the wall as if turned by unseen hands.

Stories of the "Rosenheim spook" began to appear in the national press which brought the case to the attention of Professor Hans Bender of the Institute of Paranormal Research at Freiburg. Bender's investigation revealed that the surges of current and other disturbances only occurred when Adam's clerk, Anne-Marie Schaberl, was present in the office and furthermore, the lights were seen to swing whenever she walked underneath them. As for the telephone calls to the speaking clock, Anne-Marie admitted that she had been so bored that she had taken to watching the clock obsessively, wishing that the day would end. Bender concluded that Anne-Marie was unconsciously generating psychokinetic energy to an abnormal degree due to her frustration. The scientific establishment poured scorn on this explanation, but the fact remained that when she left the office to undergo a series of tests at the institute, the activity abruptly ceased.

Bender considered Anne-Marie's intense, neurotic personality to be typical of that which attracts poltergeist activity and suspected that his subject would prove to have psychic abilities. In the initial tests she showed no signs of telepathic talent, but after the professor questioned her about a traumatic illness that had kept her in a plaster cast for a year her scores increased dramatically. Emotional stress appeared to stimulate her production of psychic energy, although without a focus into which it could be channelled it had simply been discharged into the atmosphere resulting in the "poltergeist" phenomenon.

When she returned to Adam's office the disturbances resumed, forcing the solicitor to terminate her employment. The same disturbing activity occurred at her next job and again at the next where a man was killed in a bizarre accident. Anne-Marie was blamed for the death by the superstitious staff and she was forced to move on. Things deteriorated further when her fiancé broke off their engagement citing the fact that every time he took her bowling the electronic scoring system would go haywire as soon as she walked in. It was only after she married another man and had a family of her own that the spontaneous psychokinetic activity ceased.

PSYCHOKINETIC POWER

THE POTENTIAL OF the human mind for creating such phenomena was ably demonstrated by Soviet psychic Nina Kulagina in a series of laboratory tests conducted in 1970. Nina was wired up to a recording apparatus which showed that certain changes took place when she was asked to perform paranormal feats (such as stopping the heartbeat of a frog or separating the yolk from the white of an egg without touching the container in which it had been placed). Scientists noticed that the electrical activity in her brain increased to an abnormal degree and her pulse rate rose from a healthy 70 beats per minute to an unprecedented 240. Moreover, the magnetic field surrounding her increased substantially to the point at which it merged with the electrical force of the machine to produce a single fluctuating rhythm on the monitoring equipment. When this peak was reached she was able to move small distant objects at will under the watchful eyes of the scientists. At such times she could be described as being in a state of nervous tension similar to that of individuals who are often found to be the epicentre of poltergeist activity. It would appear that psychokinetic disturbances might occur as a result of certain psychological disorders, although it is not necessary to be under stress to produce these effects.

In another series of controlled tests conducted in 1972 a team of researchers from the Canadian Society for Psychical Research used mental energy to give life to a fictional character whom they named Philip. The group gave Philip characteristics which they meditated upon at weekly meetings until their combined and focused minds succeeded in creating a thought-form which then took on an independent existence. Philip communicated by rapping upon a table, answering questions concerning his past with one rap for "yes" and two for "no." He even levitated the table in full view of television cameras.

The creation of such entities has been a central mental discipline common to many esoteric orders through the ages and remains a part of any serious psychic work in many modern spiritual groups. However, the scientific establishment remained sceptical of the Canadian group's findings as it was impossible to substantiate their claim that they had proven the existence of psychokinesis. Others argued that they may even have been fooled by a mischievous poltergeist who had been attracted by their dabbling in the occult.

THE MALEVOLENT MONK

WHILE THOUGHT-FORMS and surges of psychokinetic energy may explain a large proportion of poltergeist activity there are many more incidents which point to the presence of malevolent spirits. One of the most convincing cases was that endured by the Pritchard family of Pontefract in Yorkshire.

Their ordeal began in 1966 when pools of water mysteriously appeared on the kitchen floor. What was curious about them—apart from the fact that none of the family admitted to having made them—was that there were no splash marks, which are virtually impossible to avoid no matter how carefully one pours liquid on to a non-absorbent surface. The spontaneous appearance of water on walls and floors is a characteristic feature of a poltergeist attack and this raises the question: could it be that psychokinetic energy condenses to form water?

In the Pritchard home, other pools of water appeared as soon as the first were mopped up, yet water board inspectors found no trace of a leak. Two days of minor manifestations followed which appeared to centre on the Pritchards' five-year-old son Philip, but then they ceased and there were no further incidents for two years. When they resumed, the Pritchards' 14-year-old daughter Diane was evidently the target.

Everything fragile in the house was systematically broken to the accompaniment of loud drumming noises which attracted crowds of bemused neighbours. Diane was repeatedly dragged out of bed by an unseen force or trapped under heavy furniture which took at least two family members to remove, but which left her without even a bruise. Curiously, the spirit only went on the rampage in the evening after Diane had returned home from school and despite the damage it caused it never actually hurt anyone. Only in the final stages did it turn nasty, dragging Diane up the staircase by the throat in full view of her father, mother and brother who rushed up the stairs and grabbed her forcing the ghost to loosen its grip. This attack left distinct red finger marks on Diane's neck, but she was otherwise unharmed. Diane's mother, Jean, later claimed that she had found huge footprints at the bottom of the stairs and that the carpet was soaking wet.

About this time the sightings began. Mr. and Mrs. Pritchard described seeing a spectral figure in the night framed in an open doorway and several independent witnesses saw shadowy glimpses of what appeared to be a hooded figure in black elsewhere in the house. On one occasion a neighbour claimed to have felt a distinct presence behind her and when she turned around, found herself confronting a tall hooded monk whose face was hidden by a cowl. An instant later it disappeared.

The final sighting occurred one evening when Mr. and Mrs. Pritchard saw a tall silhouette darken the frosted glass of the dining room door. When they looked inside the room they saw a shadowy shape sink slowly into the floor. It was the last incident in the baffling Pontefract case.

Subsequent research has unearthed the fact that the Pritchard house had been built on the site of a gallows where a Cluniac monk had been hanged for rape during the reign of Henry VIII. However, there may be more to the Pontefract "haunting" than this. Could it be that Philip and Diane created the disturbances through the unconscious use of psychokinetic energy?

Diane had been away from home at the time of the first attack so it may be assumed that if psychokinesis was the cause of the disturbances, Philip was the source of the first outburst and Diane the second.

Five is the age at which it is believed that children lose their link with the spirit world as they strengthen their hold on the physical world, thereby precipitating minor psychic disturbances. Similarly, when the second series of attacks occurred Diane was 14 and entering puberty, a period of emotional upheaval which many parapsychologists suspect is the prime cause of poltergeist activity. Perhaps it was significant that Diane admitted to being only mildly upset by the phenomenon at first, as if she unconsciously suspected that she might be the source.

The outbreak of poltergeist activity may then have been caused by recurrent spontaneous psychokinesis and the spirit might have been an anonymous, featureless thought-form, created and animated by the family's fear (to a degree where it could be seen by other people).

Dr. A.R.G. Owen, author of *Can We Explain the Poltergeist?*, suggests that the phenomenon may be what he calls a "conversion neurosis" in which anxiety triggers the energy bursts which produce loud noises, electrical faults and the movement of objects. Furthermore, such activities cease because poltergeist activity "is not the disease but the cure."

In 1980 the writer Colin Wilson, an expert on the para-normal and an avowed sceptic on the subject of spirits, vis-ited the Pritchard family and interviewed other witnesses, including the neighbours. Their testimonies, together with tape recordings of the violent banging noises and contem-porary newspaper reports, finally convinced Wilson that this was a genuine case of poltergeist activity by "an inde-pendent entity." He later wrote: "The evidence points clearly in that direction and it would be simple dishonesty not to admit it."

But if the Pontefract poltergeist was a restless spirit why did it disappear after making a few fleeting appear-ances and not make any demands to be laid to rest or avenged? If it had been a thought-form it would, in time, have disintegrated into the ether just as the shadowy shape in the dining room is said to have done. But could a thought-form have been strong enough to drag Diane up the stairs?

There is a third possibility which is that bursts of psy-chokinetic energy might appear like flares in the darkness of the astral plane to which earthbound spirits or elemen-tal life-forms are attracted in accordance with the univer-sal law of "like attracts like." When the source of the psychic disturbance becomes emotionally stable or less anxious, the spirits simply drift away.

21

ANGELS

WHEN A FURTIVE, middle-aged man approached Blessed Breet, a provincial lay preacher in one of Holland's most notorious red-light districts, and asked for a word in private, Breet expected to be threatened with violence if he continued his missionary work in the town. Instead, when the two were alone, the man made a confession which Breet was to include in his memoirs and repeat to anyone who feared that they were alone in the world.

The stranger said that he was now a reformed character who felt the need to unburden himself of a guilty secret if he was to complete his conversion and find absolution.

The stranger freely confessed that 20 years earlier, in the early 1900s, he and another man had plotted to kill the preacher because his weekly prayer meetings were having a detrimental effect on their business. Local men feared that they might be seen in the company of prostitutes by their neighbours who were attending the meetings and several prostitutes were even expressing a serious interest in converting to Christianity.

So one night the stranger had knocked on Breet's door and asked him to attend a dying man at the other end of town. He told him the address, but by the time Breet had dressed, the man had disappeared. So the preacher set off alone. It proved to be a false alarm and Breet had thought nothing more about it until now. Then the stranger admitted that he and his accomplice had been waiting in the shadows to attack Breet and drown him in the canal. But they had abandoned their plan when they saw the preacher with two companions.

"But I was on my own the whole way," said Breet in disbelief.

"My friend and I clearly saw someone on each side of you," repeated the stranger.

"Then the Lord must have sent two angels to keep me safe," said Breet with satisfaction.

I have described some of my own experiences with the angels in *Angels—A Piatkus Guide* but the following story was not included because I considered it too personal at the time of writing.

Shortly before Christmas 1990 I was feeling very low after having ended a difficult relationship. I was beginning to despair of finding someone who I could settle down with and, in a mood of resignation, I asked the angels to send me the person that was "right" for me. I didn't perform any particular rite of the kind that New Age "angel experts" advise us to do when we seek to communicate with these celestial beings. I simply entered a meditative state and asked for help, believing that if I sought lasting happiness rather than an idealised image all would come right in the end. Whether my prayer, if I can call it that, reached the angels, or God, or whether it simply effected a profound change in my attitude at an unconscious level I cannot say, but it worked. A year to the very day that I had asked the angels for help I met my future wife under very strange circumstances.

She knocked at my front door having travelled all the way from Germany on the off-chance of meeting me. She had read my books and seen my photograph and felt compelled to meet me, although she had no idea what my personal circumstances might be. Within 18 months we were married. I no longer believe in coincidence.

THERE ARE THOUSANDS of similar stories which have been reported in recent times, offering proof that angelic encounters are not the exclusive preserve of biblical prophets, saints or mystics. In the digital age the subject of angels might seem an anachronism, and yet there are numerous websites to be found on the internet describing modern miracles and life-enhancing encounters with benign supernatural beings the world over. Many of the individuals whose lives have been transformed by these encounters have no religious convictions, or even a passing interest in the paranormal. They cannot explain why they were "chosen," nor can they fully understand what it was that touched their lives. They only know that they have been transformed by a profound spiritual experience which cannot be conveyed in words.

SPIRITUAL SAMARITANS

THESE DAYS ANGELS rarely appear adorned with the traditional halo and wings. Instead they usually materialise in human form like good Samaritans and it is only later that those they have helped begin to question the uncanny coincidence which brought them out of danger.

In her account of the 1929 Arab uprising, *Appointment in Jerusalem*, journalist Lydia Prince recounts the day that she was trapped in an Arab house in a section of the city that was under fire from both Arabs and Jews. She had rescued a Jewish baby, but was fearful that it would die of thirst as the water supply to the house had been cut off. She was afraid of venturing outside, but believed that she had no choice if the baby was to have a chance of survival. She quietly prayed for heavenly protection and then, fearing the worst, she stepped out into the street. Suddenly there was silence. Not a shot was fired, although she knew that snipers had previously shown no compassion for women and children. In the uncanny silence she walked from street to street carrying the child until she came to a barricade that was too high to climb. In despair she sat down, not knowing what to do next. At that moment a young man appeared dressed in European clothes and, without saying a word, he gently took the child from her. He led them over the barricade and through deserted streets which had earlier resounded with gunfire. Still not a shot was heard. After negotiating a labyrinth of rubble-strewn streets he stopped by the door of an anonymous-looking house and passed the baby back to Lydia. Then, still without a word, he left them. It was then that Lydia recognised the house as the home of a friend. Fortunately the friend was there and she helped Lydia take care of the baby. The friend could not recall a man fitting the description ever having visited her house and the pair were left to conclude that Lydia's prayer had been answered in the most practical way.

A MODERN MIRACLE

ANGELS DO NOT always materialise, but in such cases their actions leave little doubt that a celestial agency was at work. Such a case was reported by William Porter of Englewoods, California in a 1983 issue of *Guideposts*, an American publication specialising in reports of angelic encounters.

William and his wife were visiting his parents when they heard their 2½-year-old daughter Helen cry out from the garden at the back of the house. They raced round to find her standing on the stone path, in great distress and dripping wet. She had evidently fallen into her grandparents' fish pond. It was only after her father had got over the shock that he realised the toddler could not have scrambled out of the pool by herself. It was 7 feet in diameter and 4 feet deep. Moreover, they had found the child 20 feet from the pool and there were no footprints between the pool and the path. The only water on the flagstones was the puddle in which the child was standing. Initially the child said nothing about the incident, but when she was older she recalled being pulled from the water by a figure in white who left as soon as her parents entered the garden.

ANGELIC ENCOUNTERS

NOT ALL ANGELIC encounters are as dramatic as these. Some appear simply to offer comfort in times of bereavement or distress. But for whatever reason they appear they are quite distinct from other supernatural experiences in three important respects.

The first is that these benign celestial beings invariably bring reassurance at a time of crisis. They usually convey the life-affirming message that the difficulties and losses we experience are necessary to our understanding and that ultimately all will be well.

Secondly, having been reminded of their true nature, the individual is profoundly affected by it for the rest of their lives, perceiving the physical world as a reflection of a greater reality.

The third characteristic of an angelic encounter is that their presence is nearly always accompanied by an aura of unconditional love and compassion which will often bring even the most down-to-earth person to tears when they recall the incident, even if it is years later.

In short, those who encounter an angel are touched to the very core of their being, and no rational explanation can diminish the experience.

One theory states that an angel might be a projection of the witness's own unconscious created by fatigue or stress. For that reason some encounters have been dismissed as typical doppelganger hallucinations, but the clinical definition of the phenomenon still only allows for a partial apparition of a ghostly transparency. Doppelgangers generally do not appear in a solid and life-like form, nor do they act independently, as did those beings which I have described.

ANGELIC INTERVENTION

IT IS HARD for humans to understand why the angelics might intervene to save one life and not another. It is my understanding that they are continuously trying to communicate with us, but few of us listen to the small voice within. Either we distrust our intuition or we are too preoccupied with our own thoughts to hear them.

Unless people have a personal experience of the angelics they also find it difficult to believe that they exist, primarily because they may not have received a response to their own requests for help. However, esoteric teachings state that the purpose of each life is to learn from experience and we can only do that if we have free will. If we know that every plea for help will bring the angels to rescue us and set things right then we will come to rely on them and cease to function as discriminating and resourceful individuals. However, it is often the case that when a person has done their best and exhausted all the options, then assistance will be given unconditionally and with love.

ANGELS AND DEMONS

IT IS UNDERSTANDABLE that many people assume that if angels exist, then so too must demons, or some form of conscious evil entity. But is it not more likely that the invisible realms reflect the hierarchy to be found in nature on the physical plane which is expressed in a multitude of forms from single-celled creatures to humankind? Supernatural phenomena are defined as anything beyond the ordinary, which is not the same as being contrary to nature.

Therefore one could imagine the celestial hierarchy as being comprised of continually evolving forms, rather than good or malevolent entities, the highest form being the angelics who are traditionally the closest beings to the Creator.

As I noted in *Angels—A Piatkus Guide*:

> "The existence of angels does not automatically signify the existence of demons. If angels are the highest form of discarnate beings surely they are complemented by lower, undeveloped forms and not necessarily by conscious beings of equal strength but of a contrary nature."

The word "demon" is actually a corruption of the Greek word *daemon* which translates simply as spirit or deity. Perhaps that is why we have an impressive record of angelic encounters through the centuries but no credible accounts of encounters with devils and demons. Our history has certainly witnessed evil acts, but in each case these appear to have been a manifestation of our own inhumanity—the shadow side of the psyche which has been separated from the source and is unconscious of its true or divine nature. If this is the case, then we have nothing to fear but our own shadows.

22

GHOSTS, GUIDES AND SPIRITS

IN 1998 AN opinion poll survey conducted by ICM revealed that 52 per cent of the population of the UK believe in life after death. Of those questioned, 13 per cent claimed to have seen a ghost, making it one of the most common forms of paranormal experience. However, none of these witnesses described having seen a malevolent hooded figure of the kind that haunts clichéd horror fiction, nor did they hear the blood-curdling screams and clanking chains which were once typical of fictional phantoms.

In reality the experience is rarely frightening. Most apparitions look solid and few acknowledge the presence of the living. It is only after they have faded, or have been identified as someone who has died, that the witness is unsettled by the thought that there might be more to reality than met the eye.

The considerable amount of documented sightings by respectable and reliable witnesses would make it difficult for even the staunchest sceptic to deny the existence of ghosts. However, the huge amount of material and the variety of experiences recorded has confused the public and the majority of paranormal investigators as to the true nature of the phenomenon. It would seem that it is no longer a question of whether or not ghosts exist, but of distinguishing between the different forms of apparitions and explaining their significance. It is my understanding that there are four types of apparition, if we exclude thought-forms, elementals and angels for the reason that they are discarnate entities and not the spirits of living or deceased human beings.

PHANTASMS

THE FIRST TYPE of apparition is not a ghost at all, but a phantasm of the living. These apparitions are projections of a living person's image and include doppelgangers, phantom forerunners and crisis apparitions. They are dealt with separately on pages 207–219.

SPIRIT GUIDES

THE SECOND CATEGORY of apparition are known as spirit guides. These highly evolved souls are thought to have chosen to periodically return to the earth plane to assist with our spiritual development. Each of us is said to have one, if not two, who guide and protect us as far as they are able, primarily through the inner voice of intuition. The more we learn to trust such feelings, the stronger will be their influence in our lives. A guide may stay with one person with whom it feels an affinity for much of that person's life, or for as long as necessary in order to see them through a particular stage of their development, after which another guide may take over. Spirit guides are usually only seen with the inner vision by psychics, although some people may glimpse them during critical times in their lives and interpret the vision as having been of their guardian angel, which is, in effect, what they are.

ECHOES OF THE DECEASED

THE THIRD TYPE of apparition is merely an impression left in the ether by the deceased which any of us may tune in to if we are psychically sensitive or our defences are down due to stress or exhaustion. These "echoes" can be particularly strong if the deceased's passing was charged with emotion of any kind, particularly guilt or violence. This type of apparition is harmless as it is without consciousness, although it can prove unsettling for those who are sensitive to its agitated vibrations, or who find the image of the deceased upsetting.

One of the first and most convincing cases of this kind in modern times was reported to the Society for Psychical Research, which was established in 1882 by a distinguished group of Cambridge scholars for the purpose of studying paranormal phenomena in a scientific manner.

Six weeks after the death of a certain Captain Towns, his son-in-law, Charles Lett, wrote to the society describing the morning that his father-in-law's ghost had appeared before the whole family. Mrs. Lett and a friend were the first to see what they described as a life-sized portrait of the captain reflected in the polished surface of a wardrobe.

He looked pale and drawn and was dressed in a grey flannel jacket. While they stared in disbelief, the captain's daughter entered the room and before either woman had time to speak she cried out: "Good gracious! Do you see Papa?"

A passing housemaid was called in and before she could be asked to verify what the others had seen she exclaimed: "Oh Miss! The Master!" While the image remained, clear but impassive, other servants were called to identify the apparition. Finally, Mrs. Towns was sent for and in her desperation to prove for herself that her husband survived in the realm of spirit she reached out to touch him. The image immediately faded and never reappeared. The case was later included in one of the earliest surveys of the subject, *Human Personality and Its Survival of Bodily Death* (1895), by the pioneer of psychical research, F.W.H. Myers. It was Myers's conclusion that apparitions such as that of Captain Towns were manifestations of "persistent personal energy," which is as good a description of a ghost as one is likely to find.

RESTLESS SPIRITS

THE FOURTH TYPE of apparition is the restless spirit of the dead. Though these spirits are rarely able to exert their influence on the material world, or cause physical harm to the living, their presence can prove distressing until they are "laid to rest." Some of these spirits may have passed into the higher realms, but may choose to manifest in order to communicate with a loved one that they have left behind.

One of the most unusual cases of this kind that Myers

claimed to have unearthed during his research was that of a travelling salesman who was "visited" by the spirit of his sister who had died nine years before. The girl appeared healthy and happy, but the brother was left with a feeling of unease. Although the vision lasted only a few moments he had noticed a detail that puzzled him even more than the apparition itself. There was a small scratch on her right cheek which he did not remember seeing while she was alive. Later, when he related his experience to his mother she broke down and described how she had accidentally scratched her daughter's face with her ring while preparing the body for burial. Curiously, the mother died two weeks after the son's visit which suggests that the purpose of the apparition might have been to encourage him to visit his mother before she too passed away.

Esoteric tradition states that the astral, or etheric body (in which the soul is encased like a seed in a shell), moulds itself after the physical body and it is this luminous projection of the personality that distinguishes a ghost, or impression, from a spirit. It is the plasticity of this subtle body of finer matter, incidentally, that accounts for the deceased being able to appear younger than they had been at the moment of death.

In normal circumstances, the personality's acceptance of death—which comes with the freedom from the physical body and an irresistible attraction to the light of the heavenly realm—will allow it to cast off the astral body like a snake sheds its skin and ascend into the higher dimensions of spirit. However, in rare cases the deceased can become earthbound, either because they are fettered to the physical world through emotional attachment, or because they are simply not aware that they are dead. Perhaps in life they were obsessively preoccupied with routine, or mundane tasks, and so after death they would exist in a somnambulant state until they came to a realisation that they have no lasting influence in the physical world (for example, their tasks are never completed). In time they will awaken from their dream of life and depart for the higher realms.

Less fortunate are those who wander between the worlds in a hell of their own making created by negative emotions such as hate, fear and jealousy, or through addiction to drink or drugs. In the past, the onerous task of laying these unquiet spirits to rest was given to priests who would perform an exorcism. These days, an increasing number of psychics and healers have dedicated themselves to "rescuing" souls and guiding them gently into the light.

BETTY SHINE

BRITAIN'S MOST HIGHLY respected and influential medium is Betty Shine, whose remarkable life story and extraordinary encounters with the unpredictable powers of the paranormal do not appear to have unsettled her in the least. Her numerous out-of-body excursions to higher dimensions, life-long encounters with spirit entities and personal experiences of the unlimited healing powers of the mind have convinced her that we all have the ability to tap this hidden potential and lose our fear of the unknown. Her autobiographical books such as *Mind to Mind*, *The Infinite Mind* and *My Life as a Medium* are the ideal introduction to the world of psychic phenomena and the latent powers that we all share. But more significantly, in recalling some of the most incredible case histories ever recorded with calm detachment and compassion, she brings the world of the supernatural out of the dark fantasy realm of the *X Files*, revealing it as simply another, albeit invisible, facet of life.

The tabloid press have dubbed Betty Shine "the world's number one healer." Despite curing thousands of people around the world and introducing millions more to the extraordinary world of psychic phenomena through her five bestselling books and numerous radio and TV appearances, Betty radiates the warmth and down-to-earth good humour one would expect of a favourite aunt.

From an early age she discovered her innate ability to pass effortlessly between this world and the next. As a toddler she suffered a serious blow to her head and while recovering in hospital found herself drifting off into a heavenly dimension which she was subsequently able to visit at will whenever she needed rest and peace. As a young child she claimed she could hear the trees talking to each other and the grass growing and began to experience the freedom of astral flight. More than once she was saved from a fatal accident by an inner voice which she believed was her guardian angel. He also reassured her when she was feeling low and gave her advice about her school work. Then at the age of ten she was evacuated to the countryside to escape the Blitz. Ill-treated and alone, she found comfort in nightly visitations by shadowy spirit entities which used to march through her bedroom and disappear through the outside wall. But Betty did not exploit her marvellous gifts as her mother was deeply religious and against anything psychic. She continued to suppress her abilities until, at the age of 46 after a career as an opera singer and mineral therapist, the repressed energies threatened her health. In desperation, she turned to a medium for guidance and was told that her destiny was to be a world-renowned psychic and healer—a destiny she was at first very reluctant to believe or pursue.

> "We are all psychic, but actually knowing that you are opens the mind to the cosmic energies which will come in and do the job. You can't come to any harm by opening up for the simple reason that like attracts like. It's a universal law. If you are a 'good' person you will only attract those forces which are there waiting to help you. All this secrecy and insistence on special practices comes from the simple fact that most mediums don't want you to know how easy it is! Most so-called occult philosophy boils down to simple common sense."

So, is there nothing to fear "out there" after all?

> "Well, let me put it this way: we are both God and the Devil. The whole universe is composed of positive and negative energies. Sometimes there is a mind behind them and sometimes it's just an accumulation of energy, but you must remember that you are battling against a formidable power when you deal with energies focused by the human mind. Whatever you give out joins like-thoughts out there in the universal mind and will multiply and come back at you. And if your thoughts are negative they will invariably come back to you when you are at your lowest ebb. That's why people who think negatively appear to get caught up in the momentum of an ever-descending spiral of what the ordinary person would perceive as bad luck. But they have created their own condition. They blame the whole bloody world instead of themselves. When you recognise that, you can break free and take control of your own life."

There may not be a separate evil being out there, but Betty has had many frightening experiences with negative entities which she has had to deal with.

On one occasion she was giving healing to a woman in her mid-50s when she saw a dark entity overshadow her patient and heard it say: "I will never leave her, she is mine." As soon as she began praying for protection Betty saw a bright white light appear behind it, putting the figure into silhouette. It was clearly a man and as he was pulled away by some unseen force in the light he screamed. The woman covered her ears, though she later claimed that she hadn't actually heard the scream, but had acted instinctively. After the entity had disappeared the woman told Betty that she had been married to a possessive, sadistic man in South Africa 30 years before, but had eventually plucked up enough courage to escape to England. Unfortunately, he had followed her there and plagued her for years before dying from a heart attack on her doorstep. After his death she remarried but still felt pursued and was thoroughly depressed. A few weeks after the exorcism the woman returned to Betty's healing centre radiant and relieved, finally free of the black cloud she had felt had been smothering her for years.

But not all the exorcisms were successful. Betty was unable to help several of her patients because she sensed that these "victims" were as negative as the entities they had attracted and concluded that they probably "deserved each other."

Such stories might deter those wishing to develop their own psychic abilities, but Betty received a valuable insight into the nature of evil from one of her unseen "gurus" which put these beings in their place. He told her that life in the spiritual dimension mirrors our own and we should therefore treat unpleasant entities in the same way that we would treat irritating and unwelcome visitors. Ignore them and turn your thoughts to higher and more pleasant matters.

"Recognising negative influences weakens the life-force and makes one vulnerable," he told her. Consequently, Betty doesn't now believe in exotic and elaborate rituals of exorcism. Her tried and trusted method is characteristically down-to-earth and guarantees to send any evil entity back where it belongs.

"I just tell them to bugger off!" she laughs.

23

LAYERS OF THE SOUL

WHETHER WE PROFESS an interest in the paranormal or not, we all share a fear of death to differing degrees and a fascination with what might lie beyond. Our attitude to the biggest mystery of all determines the way that we live our lives, for death is the one certain thing in an ever-changing world. It is only the timing and manner of our passing that is unknown and it is this unpredictable aspect which prevents many of us from facing the inevitable until we are forced to do so. However, in esoteric traditions and in the mystic East, death is seen not as the end but as one stage in the evolution of the soul, a transformation as natural as that which sees the butterfly emerging from the cocoon and, by all accounts, far less traumatic than birth.

All major religions and philosophical systems have at their core the idea that each of us possesses an immortal soul or "spirit double" which survives the death of the physical body. In the ancient world it was more common to envisage the soul as being clothed in a series of subtle bodies, like Russian dolls, each made of increasingly finer matter appropriate to the various levels of the inner plane. This was the concept behind the ancient Egyptian practice of placing the mummified body of the pharaoh inside sarcophagi of increasing refinement, and it remains central to the belief of many modern esoteric groups and Eastern philosophies including Buddhism.

It is thought that at the highest level, the soul, or divine essence, is pure consciousness which acquires its subtle protective layers during its descent through the higher worlds, a process mythologised as the Fall, or exile from the Garden of Eden. The soul assumes a recognisable form as it passes through the second world, the world of spirit, then it wraps itself in the plastic-like matter of the third level, the astral plane, before taking on physical form in the densest of the four worlds, our own.

OUT-OF-BODY EXPERIENCES

THE BEST EVIDENCE that we have for life after death is the numerous accounts of out-of-body experiences, or OBEs, and the universal nature of those experiences. From a number of recent statistical surveys it has been estimated that as many as one person in five in the West has had a conscious out-of-body experience which they can recall in vivid detail upon waking and which they describe as being quite distinct from a dream. It is believed that we all experience the phenomenon periodically during the deepest phases of sleep when the physical body is relaxed and the conscious mind is at rest. It is then that our astral, or etheric body, can float free of the physical shell on the end of an umbilical-like cord of etheric matter. While we dream it hovers just inches above the body, but it can be directed to follow the unconscious will to distant locations in the physical world at the speed of thought.

All of us can recall the sensation of flying during a particularly vivid dream and of falling just before waking up as the astral body returns to the physical shell, but many people tend to dismiss the experience as just a dream because they cannot conceive of the idea that consciousness can be separated from the body.

Involuntary out-of-body experiences are often triggered by extreme exhaustion, illness, unendurable pain or the use of soporific drugs including general anaesthetics which desensitise the body, but which do not always result in unconsciousness. A typical example of an involuntary OBE was that experienced by the American artist and celebrated psychic Ingo Swann who, at the age of two and a half, watched from a third person perspective as a surgeon removed his tonsils and popped them into a jar. When Swann regained consciousness he was able to recall the details of the operation, including the fact that the surgeon had cursed when the scalpel had slipped and cut the tongue. Swann also correctly pointed out where the surgeon had placed the jar which was hidden from view behind rolls of tissue.

As an adult, Swann was able to leave his body at will to explore distant locations and describe hidden objects, a talent which was tested under strict laboratory conditions at Stanford University (see page 159). Swann's out-of-body experiences indicate that there is no limit to the distance that the astral body can travel within our physical dimension. He claimed to have projected his consciousness to Mercury and returned with details of the planet's magnetic field and other features which were unknown to scientists at the time, but which were subsequently confirmed by the Mariner 10 probe.

THE TIMELESS ZONE

ONE OF THE most credible descriptions of the astral experience was given by an eminent academic, Sir Auckland Geddes, a professor of anatomy, in a lecture to members of the Royal Medical Society in 1937. Geddes accredited the experience to an anonymous physician, but it is believed that it was his own and that he invented the other man for fear of exposing himself to ridicule by the medical establishment.

According to Geddes, the physician was lying in bed critically ill when he had the sensation that his consciousness was separating into two distinct perspectives; one purely mental and the other focused in his physical body. He felt this physical centre dissolve until he was left observing his feverish body with interest, but no emotion, from the other side of the room. The astral body in which he now found himself could evidently direct its attention to any location in the world at will, for material boundaries and distance had no reality for it. In this fourth dimension the only reality was the current moment. In order to convey this other reality, the anonymous physician described the human brain as the physical receptacle of a "psychic stream" which permeates these interpenetrating dimensions. When we are focused on the physical world we tune in to the lowest frequency of vibration, but when we raise our consciousness through meditation, or in response to an uplifting stimulus, we can become aware of these other realities as if we had tuned in to a higher wavelength.

In the fourth dimension, the physician became aware of the multi-coloured auras of energy surrounding those living in the physical world whom he could still see and hear clearly. In effect, he had become a living apparition although those whom he observed were too preoccupied to notice him or sense his presence.

Before he could explore further a friend entered his room and, finding him in a comatose state, immediately telephoned for a doctor. At that same moment, the physician saw the doctor receiving the emergency call and then witnessed the efforts made to bring him back to life. As he was drawn back into his body he became "intensely annoyed" about having to be confined once again in the flesh. "I was so interested and was just beginning to understand where I was and what I was seeing," he explained.

THE NATURE OF THE MIND

IT WAS CLEARLY difficult for Geddes to put the sensation into words for there was no equivalent of this perspective in everyday experience. The closest one could come to it would be to draw parallels with the sensation of timelessness, heightened awareness and detachment which is sought during meditation. It would seem that time only exists in the physical world because it is a man-made concept devised to measure growth and change. For practical purposes and to give the mortal ego a (false) sense of security, we need to think of life as a linear progression, but the natural phenomenon of death and rebirth demonstrates that life is cyclical. Our essence, and that of all existence, be it animate or inanimate, is immortal. It is immortal because it is pure consciousness and consciousness is energy. Even matter is only energy vibrating at a lower frequency to give the illusion of form. When a person experiences an OBE and travels in the astral plane, they intuitively "know" this to be true.

When in the astral body we have no impact on the physical world as we exist on a higher frequency in the space in between the atoms. This is why ghosts appear to pass through solid objects. It is the apparent solidity of the physical world that makes it possible to measure change and for us to think in terms of a past, present and future. But we only have to think of the future or recall the past to appreciate that the mind exists beyond the restrictions of time and space and that if our true nature is indeed pure consciousness we only have to raise our awareness beyond the physical to perform all manner of paranormal feats.

NEAR-DEATH EXPERIENCES

OUT-OF-BODY experiences and near-death experiences (NDEs) are often confused, but they are not the same thing. Both involve projection of the astral body, but an OBE is normally limited to an exploration of the physical world and, in rare cases of the dream-like astral dimension, while in an NDE the astral traveller is drawn to the boundary that divides the astral from the higher worlds, and there catches a glimpse of the heavenly realm.

Dr. Raymond Moody, an American physician who coined the term "near-death experience," published one of the first scientific studies into the phenomenon, *Life After Life*, in 1975, in which he compared 150 first-hand accounts, many of them from people who were resuscitated after having been declared clinically dead.

To Moody's surprise the descriptions were uncannily consistent, suggesting that his patients had all shared the same experience, although they came from a wide variety of backgrounds and subscribed to different beliefs. Some had been firm disbelievers in the existence of life after death, and yet they described a very similar experience and were clearly as profoundly affected as the others.

Dr. Moody identified a number of common elements, which it appears have been shared by thousands of other individuals who have made similar claims in subsequent studies, although not every person experienced these events in the same sequence. However, in almost every case the process of death was characterised by an absence of pain and an overwhelming sensation of serenity which allayed all fears at the moment of separation, even in cases of violent or sudden death. Many patients described the ecstasy they felt on finding themselves floating free of their physical body and of watching as the doctors and nurses frantically attempted to revive them. Several recall trying in vain to tell them not to bother, that they were happy to be rid of the burden of their sick or injured body, but nobody seemed aware of their presence. Curiously, the "deceased" could hear everything that the medical teams said during the crises and were later able to repeat it. They were also able to describe precisely what had happened while they were technically "dead," details which were subsequently verified by the hospital staff. Many spent what they later learnt had been several minutes out of the body during which they were drawn down a long, dark tunnel to emerge in a pastoral landscape where they were welcomed by deceased friends and relatives. There was an innate sense of familiarity about this place and a feeling of "coming home."

HEAVEN AND HELL

ONE OF THE best and most detailed descriptions of the
heavenly realm was given to American psychic researcher
David Wheeler who subsequently published the account in
Journey to the Other Side (1977). The man whom Wheeler
identifies as Kenneth G. "died" from a heart attack shortly
after being admitted to hospital. The doctor who attended
him later admitted that had he not known the man's daughter personally he would not have considered trying to
revive him, for the body was already showing signs of
rigor mortis. "He was as dead as anyone I have ever seen,"
said the doctor. "I saw no real hope, but decided to go
ahead as though I thought there was."

Kenneth G. returned from the dead against all the odds
and with no ill effects or brain damage, although all the
medical textbooks say that it is not possible to make a full
recovery once the brain and vital functions have ceased for
more than a few seconds. But the most extraordinary
aspect of his experience was the description he gave his
doctor of the land "on the other side."

> "I found myself in the most enchanting place you could
> ever visit. The beauty was far beyond anything that I
> have ever seen before in my life. It was so luxuriant that
> there is absolutely no way to express to you the intense
> enjoyment I felt with the place."

He described a landscape of low hills and endless rolling
plains within a vast and verdant valley. He had the sensation of drifting gently down as if he was suspended on the
end of a parachute and he made a landing in a meadow of
tall grass which came up to his waist. From here he could

see animals, trees and a profusion of exotic flowers, the like of which he had never seen before.

> "It was a delightful sensation. Then I saw that this meadow went on for ever. I saw dense forests in the far distance . . . The only word I seem to be able to use to talk about that place is 'beautiful.'"

For what seemed like a few minutes he stood in that waist-high grass, looking around in wonder and listening to the rustle of the grass in the breeze. At first there was no other sound and then he heard a faint voice which gradually grew louder. There was nobody in sight, but Kenneth recognised the voice as being that of his father who had died ten years before.

> "'What is he doing here?' I thought to myself. 'Here I am in a strange meadow. I don't know where I am, and my dead father is calling to me.' I accepted things as they were—what else could I do? The voice kept faintly telling me: 'Kenneth, don't be afraid. Do not worry, I have come to help you with your journey. Don't be afraid of this. I've helped others.'"

The next moment he heard laughter from across the meadow and in the distance he saw children playing in what appeared to be an amusement park. It was like the one at Coney Island that he remembered visiting as a child. As he looked he felt drawn towards them; the mere wish being sufficient to bring him closer. Their faces were strangely familiar.

"All my old playmates were there, just like they were 60
years ago . . . None of them noticed me; they continued
to play in the amusement park as we had done half a
century ago . . . I was a little boy again, reliving [my]
youth . . . God, it was beautiful!

"Death seemed to have blended the hereafter with the
fondest memories I carried through life. I know I went to
heaven with my most cherished childhood memories . . .
How wrong it was for them to bring me back from such
a wonderful place."

The description of this celestial garden with its vivid,
unworldly colours invites comparison with the traditional
images of heaven, but it cannot easily be explained away
as a mass hallucination resulting from cultural condition-
ing. Paradise has been described in quite different terms by
various traditions. For example, the Buddhist tradition
speaks of various heavens as being symbolic of states of
consciousness. The heaven known as Indra is described as
being perceived by the individual soul in terms of a lush
pastoral garden populated by exotic birds and where the
trees change their appearance with the passing seasons.
The Muslim paradise (al-Jannah) is described in similar
terms with beautiful gardens flowing with streams of milk,
wine and honey. Every material comfort is provided in
palatial surroundings and all the immortal inhabitants are
treated as kings. But even people of the same faith would
be expected to envisage heaven in the light of their own
imagination as opposed to agreeing on so many details as
these individuals have done.

At some point in the journey the "deceased" encounters
a formless being of light which some are inclined on their
return to interpret as God, Jesus or an angel, depending on

their beliefs, although most accept it as being the embodiment of love rather than an identifiable entity. From the light a voice asks if the individual is ready to die which has the effect of reminding them of their responsibilities or of unfinished business on earth. This is usually sufficient to draw them back into their body with a firm determination not to waste another moment of their life. Some have spoken of being asked by the light what they had done with their life, although this was not said with any sense of judgement, after which they reviewed the events of their life in a series of flashbacks. From the descriptions it sounds as if each person is judged by their own conscience, or higher self, rather than a celestial court, although some have recalled having to live through certain significant events once again only this time with the perspective and feelings of those they have wronged.

In contrast, descriptions of hell are few and far between, with the few that we have sounding more like a nightmare created by the disturbed mind of the deceased than a real place in another dimension. One woman would say no more than: "If you leave here a tormented soul, you will be a tormented soul over there too," while a widower who had attempted suicide in his despair said cryptically: "I didn't go where [my wife] was. I went to an awful place . . . I immediately saw what a mistake I had made." The realisation was evidently enough to snap him back to consciousness.

Recent research into negative NDEs by Tony Lawrence, a lecturer in psychology at Coventry University, and others has concluded that such experiences are very rare compared to positive NDEs and that they usually involve what Lawrence calls "an absence of experience" or a feeling of being dragged down into a pit. Both sound more like a nightmare in which a sensation of helplessness, disorientation and despair manifests as disturbing images and emotions, rather than a real experience, for they have none of the substance or detail of the positive NDE experience.

Although sections of the scientific community and medical staff with first-hand experience of treating the terminally ill appear to be coming round to a begrudging acceptance of the phenomenon, the medical establishment generally tends to dismiss such testimonies as hallucinations caused by anoxia (a lack of oxygen in the brain) or the side-effects of drugs. However, hallucinations are random and senseless and cannot account for the consistency of the experiences that have been described. Moreover, hallucinations cannot be produced when the patient is clinically dead for the brain is then inactive. EEG traces which measure electrical impulses from the brain are invariably seen to be flat and unresponsive during the period when the patient claims to have been out of their body.

Whatever cynics may say, the fact remains that such experiences have been proven to have a profound psychological effect on those who claim to have experienced them. People return to the physical world as less intense, more compassionate and more easy-going individuals than they were before, having not only lost their fear of the unknown, but having gained a greater appetite for life.

I BEGAN THIS book by remarking that I hoped it would be different from other titles on a similar theme. I trust that I have fulfilled this aim, but of more importance I hope that I have managed to take some of the fear out of the unknown.

Fear is the most significant factor in limiting our understanding. It is more than a reluctance to venture into the dark. Fear is a subtle and insidious parasite that sucks our self-confidence and drains us of the vitality that fuels our curiosity. It expresses itself in the various conspiracy theories which encourage us to suspect our own shadows and in the need to credit extraterrestrials with the construction of the foundations of civilisation. This belief undermines human ambition, imagination and achievement.

There are certainly things to be feared, but it is my conclusion that these are all of human origin. We are not at the mercy of ghosts or the gods, but of our own emotions. Once we accept that we are at the centre of our own universe and have the power to create our own reality, only then can we realise our true nature and begin to become the gods that, in essence, we really are.

BIBLIOGRAPHY

Bonewitz, R. *The Cosmic Crystal Spiral*. Element Books, Shaftesbury, 1987

Bradbury, W. *Into the Unknown*. London, 1983

Campbell, E. and Brennan, J. H. *Dictionary of Mind, Body and Spirit*. Thorsons, London, 1994

Currie, I. *Visions of Immortality*. Element Books, Shaftesbury, 1998

Hancock, G. and Faiia, S. *Heaven's Mirror*. Michael Joseph, London, 1998

Hatcher-Childress, D. *Extraterrestrial Archaeology*. Adventures Unlimited, New York, 1996

Holroyd, S. *Mysteries of the Inner Self*. London, 1981

Lovelock, J. *Gaia: The Practical Science of Planetary Medicine*. Gaia Books, London, 1991

Moolenburgh, Dr. H. C. *Meetings with Angels*. C. W. Daniel, Saffron Walden, 1992

Morehouse, D. *Psychic Warrior*. Temple Lodge Publishing, London, 1996

Picknett, L. and Prince, C. *The Stargate Conspiracy*. Little, Brown & Co, London, 1999

Randles, J. *The Paranormal Source Book*. Piatkus, London, 1999

Roland, Paul. *Kabbalah Piatkus Guide*. Piatkus, London, 1999

Roland, Paul. *Angels Piatkus Guide*. Piatkus, London, 1999

Roland, Paul. *Revelations—the Wisdom of the Ages*. Ulysses Press, 1995

Roland, Paul. *The Complete Guide to Dreams*. Hamlyn, London, 1999

Shine, B. *Mind Magic*. Corgi, London, 1996

Shine, B. *Mind to Mind*. Corgi, London, 1996

Solomon, G. *Stephen Turoff—Psychic Surgeon*. Thorsons, London, 1997

Temple, R. *The Sirius Mystery*. Arrow, London, 1998

Various (Editors of *Time-Life*) *Mysteries of the Unknown*. Time-Life Books, New York, 1997

White, M. *Life Out There*. Warner, London, 1998

White, M. *The Science of the X-Files*. Legend, London, 1996

Wilson, C. *Alien Dawn*. Virgin, London, 1998

Wilson, C. *From Atlantis to the Sphinx*. Virgin, London, 1997

Wilson, C. *Mysteries*. London, 1979

INDEX

PENGUIN PUTNAM INC.
Online

Your Internet gateway to a virtual environment with hundreds of entertaining and enlightening books from Penguin Putnam Inc.

While you're there, get the latest buzz on the best authors and books around—

Tom Clancy, Patricia Cornwell, W.E.B. Griffin, Nora Roberts, William Gibson, Robin Cook, Brian Jacques, Catherine Coulter, Stephen King, Ken Follett, Terry McMillan, and many more!

Penguin Putnam Online is located at
http://www.penguinputnam.com

PENGUIN PUTNAM NEWS

Every month you'll get an inside look at our upcoming books and new features on our site. This is an ongoing effort to provide you with the most up-to-date information about our books and authors.

Subscribe to Penguin Putnam News at
http://www.penguinputnam.com/newsletters